Expelled to a Friendlier Place

Expelled to a Friendlier Place

A Study of Effective Alternative Schools

**Martin Gold and
David W. Mann**

Ann Arbor
The University of Michigan Press

Published in the United States of America by
The University of Michigan Press and simultaneously
in Rexdale, Canada, by John Wiley & Sons Canada, Limited
Manufactured in the United States of America

1987   1986   1985   1984   4   3   2   1

Library of Congress Cataloging in Publication Data

Gold, Martin, 1931–
   Expelled to a friendlier place.

   Bibliography: p.
   Includes index.
   1. Non-formal education—United States—Case studies.
2. Problem children—Education—United States—Case
studies. 3. Deviant behavior—Case studies. I. Mann,
David W. II. Title.
LC45.4.G64   1984   371'.04   83-21792
ISBN 0-472-08046-6 (pbk.)

Preface

It gives the authors a great deal of pleasure to be able to report that there is a program to remedy an important personal and social problem that "works." After many years of applying fairly rigorous social scientific methods to the study of programs designed to remedy the self-defeating and troublesome behavior of some adolescents, and finding these programs ineffective, we have finally found a program that makes a difference. Of course, the particular kind of alternative schools that we studied is not the whole answer, and their impact, while substantial, was limited. But it is encouraging to have found that what we believed to be promising, on the basis of theory and previous evidence, fulfills its promises.

Our findings are especially encouraging to us as social scientists because they suggest that we achieved some better understanding of the causes of adolescents' disruptive and delinquent behavior. This research was grounded in theory. It was designed as much to further our understanding as it was to evaluate a program addressed to the problem of adolescent misbehavior. It was done with a commitment to the famous but seldom followed dictum of the late Kurt Lewin that "there is nothing so practical as a good theory" (1945, 129).

We note with some satisfaction that a belief in scientific method is becoming more widespread among the public, so that even religious fundamentalists have tried to invoke the aura of science (e.g., "*scientific* creationism") to advance their cause. One consequence of this change in our culture is that educators and others who conduct public programs are more frequently required to demonstrate the worth of their programs by scientifically respectable means. Our research is part of this current. We hope that the study will enrich this new tradition in its aim to do more than merely evaluate whether or not the programs were successful. We tried also to find out *why* they were successful if they were, or if they were not, why they were not. So the processes as well as the outcomes of the program were carefully researched. This is where theory was essential.

One contribution of this theoretically guided attention to process was to identify certain types of youth for whom the programs proved ineffective. This finding sheds some empirical light on the theoretical questions of types of problematic adolescents and their different origins. It also has practical implications for modifying the programs to meet needs they are not now meeting.

A study such as this one is quite complicated and therefore required the efforts of a host of people. Literally hundreds of interviews were conducted, questionnaires administered, records searched and abstracted, and hours spent observing what went on in classrooms. The study could not help but intrude on the activities of students, teachers, and staff people.

We are indebted to many individuals and organizations—too many to list, in fact—for the cooperation, assistance, and hard work which went into the Alternative Schools project. From the National Institute of Education to our individual respondents, the study would not have happened without their help. Included in the above are the school districts, administrators, counselors, and teachers we worked with, observed, and probed; the police agencies and courts which complied with our requests for (anonymous) data; the staffs of the alternative schools, generous with both time and ideas; and the staff of the project itself—a delightful and dedicated group of people. We would also like to thank our colleagues at the Institute for Social Research for their support, encouragement, and advice.

Contents

Tables and Figures

Figures

Chapter 1

Introduction

"School adjustment" invariably means students accommodating to the organization of their schools. It is not necessarily unfair for schools to insist that the students adjust. It is a crucial feature of schools preparing students for living in their society.

But some students will not—cannot—adjust, even when they've gotten as far as high school. They will not do their homework, they are inattentive in class when they go to class, they truant frequently, and worse, they interfere with other students' education by disrupting the educational process and sometimes even making the schools dangerous.

It is ironic that the success of American public education is responsible for the presence of disruptive students in the schools. The proportion of school-aged youth actually going to school in the United States has been steadily rising. Of course, this is due partly to the unsuitability and superfluity of child labor in a technologically advanced society. But it is also on account of the high value Americans place on an educated citizenry, a value enhanced by the relatively recent improvements in assuring "one person, one vote." Thus, many young people remain in school today who in the past would have "adjusted" to the educational system by leaving it. Now, the less skilled, less motivated, and less self-controlled students continue to go to school—more or less. Furthermore, law and practice have recently made it more difficult for these young people to drop out when they want to; or for educators to exclude them when they want to. It has become more incumbent upon the public schools to educate all children as much as reasonably possible regardless of the mutual unsuitability of the students and mainstream conventional schooling.

It seems plausible that this situation would result in greater disruption in the schools. Actually, however, whether the behavior of American junior and senior high schools is any worse now than earlier is not at all clear. According to the report by the National Institute of Education (NIE) on *Violent Schools–Safe Schools* (NIE 1978, 2), "the evidence from a number of studies and official sources indicates that while acts of violence and property destruction in schools increased from the early sixties to the seventies, both increases leveled off after the early 1970's." Robert J. Rubel reported in *The Unruly School* (1977) that relatively minor disorders in the classroom were more frequent in the period 1964 to 1971, but

> From about 1971 to 1975, incidents of classroom disorders seemed to decline, even though there were concurrent indications that pupil crimes were becoming more of an issue. . . . As in-school crime offense data became available for the first time in the late 1960s, the public was exposed to misrepresentation of statistics. Changes in reporting methods gave the distorted impression that incidents of student crimes increased horrendously. This study contends that whereas absolute numbers of criminal acts did go up in this period, they did not go up at anything like the range reported by most popular sources. . . . [S]uffice it to say that the percentage of assaults on teachers was relatively unchanged over time and that fires and vandalism has dramatically increased over time. (Pp. 162–63)

Furthermore, American adolescents' own confidential confessions in parallel surveys done in 1967 and 1972 demonstrated a decline from 36 percent to 27 percent ($p < .05$) of youths admitting to committing one or more chargeable offenses in school in that period (Gold and Moles 1978).

But a social problem is defined not so much by empirical reality as by the concerns of the public or by leaders of public opinion. For several years now, American educators and the public have nominated *discipline* as a major problem of our schools (Rubel 1977). The disruptive behavior of some students, especially in the secondary schools, is widely believed to be impeding the efforts of teachers to maintain enough order to impart knowledge and skills. In this sense at least, discipline in the schools is definitely a social problem. One consequence of this public concern was the establishment of a program within the National Institute of Education to study the safety of American schools and to suggest ways to improve their safety. The U.S. Congress specifically mandated a Safe Schools Study, which issued a major report in 1978 (NIE 1978). In addition to that effort, NIE supported several other studies of the problem. The research reported here was one of those. One of its aims was to bring the methods of social science to bear on the problem. However, our interest in the problem was not only practical, it was also theoretical. We believed that theory, carefully constructed on the foundation of previous evidence, would suggest promising solutions.

It seemed to us that a study of the encounter between different kinds of schools and troublesome students could advance theory in several domains of psychology—social, developmental, and personality—and recognized that it had sociological and anthropological implications as well. We believed that work on the problem of school discipline could be fruitful if it involved an interchange between the dual needs to solve a concrete social problem and to resolve some theoretical issues. A major theoretical problem for social psychology is the causes of *deviance.* The relevant interest of developmental psychology is the particular form that deviant behavior most frequently takes in adolescence and other stages of the life span. The focus of personality psychology in this study is the enduring characteristics of individuals that underlie certain kinds of deviant behavior. So the social problem was rich ore for theoretically oriented mining.

Our theoretical orientation grew out of our own research and others' on delinquent behavior in adolescence (e.g., Gold 1970; Gold and Mann 1972; Kaplan 1980; Mann 1981). Delinquency is the form of deviance most closely identified with adolescence (Gold and Petronio 1980), which is the reason for its interest to developmental psychologists. It seems to be affected by social institutions such as the family and the schools (although delinquency's reputed relationships to the economy and social class are now in doubt), so it has great relevance to social psychology. And psychologists who study the formation and maintenance of personality are interested because there are wide variations among young people in the degree to which they are delinquent, and their delinquent behavior seems to have roots in their past and is prognostic of their future (Robins 1966). Before launching this study, we had tested parts of a theory that integrated several of these psychological concerns, and with some success. Elements of the theory implicated the schools directly, so the practical problem of discipline in the schools was particularly relevant.

Our theory led us to some innovative programs with which some school systems are addressing the problem, programs that go under the generic name of *alternative schools.* One learns after only a brief scan of alternative schools that there are many different kinds of alternatives, with different philosophies, purposes, and methods. They serve a variety of students, not all of them by any means problematic. While some exist to address problems or deficiencies, others strive to open up new opportunities for their students. Alternative schools have been created for the gifted as well as the poor student, for the well-behaved as well as the disruptive. Some could be described as "permissive," others as "strict"; some concentrate on basic scholastic skills while others pursue special talents and interests; and so on. About all that alternative schools have in common is that their programs are somehow different from the curriculum followed by the large majority of the community's students.

We should point out that not every authority defines alternative schools quite this way. To Daniel L. Duke (1978, 4), "an alternative school simply is a school accessible by choice, not assignment." Vernon H. Smith, author of *Alternative Schools* (1974, 18), writes, "special-function schools that serve students who are assigned or referred without choice are not included in this definition [of 'alternative schools']." However, many of the alternative school students in this study did not attend by choice, at least, not at first. That is not the sense in which we mean "alternative."

We were specifically interested in those alternative schools designed to serve students identified as behavior problems in their conventional schools. These problems included chronic truancy, disruptive behavior, and serious delinquency. Among the many kinds of alternative schools can be found a substantial proportion with this mission. Accurate figures are not available, but authorities on alternative education indicate that approximately a third of alternative programs are designed as responses to these problems (see Arnove 1978). Within these limits, however, there is still a wide variety of approaches: disciplinarian, "back to basics," detention, behavior modification, and others (Deal and Nolan 1978).

Our immediate interest did not include just any alternative school designed for troublesome or troubled students. Our theory directed us only to programs that displayed certain characteristics which according to the theory should make these alternative schools effective in reducing disruptive and delinquent behavior. We identified schools of the requisite type and were fortunate in enlisting their participation and the cooperation of their school districts.

In brief then, this study was conducted for both theoretical and practical purposes. These two purposes were closely related. The theoretical purpose was to test a portion of a theory about the school-related causes of disruptive and delinquent behavior. The practical purpose was to determine whether a particular kind of alternative educational program is effective in reducing disruptive and delinquent behavior among secondary school students. The theory and some empirical data supporting it led us to a certain few alternative schools whose programs included features that hypothetically should make them effective.

A Partial Theory of Delinquent Behavior

To be clear about why we selected certain programs to study and why we asked the questions about them that we did, we now present the theory that guided our research.

It was our hypothesis when we began this study that certain kinds of alternative schools would reduce the delinquent behavior of their students significantly, regardless of other influences in their lives. That hypothesis certainly makes a large claim for the effectiveness of schools, especially when one considers how other influences like families, peer groups, and poverty have been theoretically identified as causes of delinquency. But our reading of the literature on delinquency and our own research have led us to formulate a theory that assigns major influence to the schools. We are not alone in this belief. Short and Strodtbeck (1965, 275) made this point in drawing implications from their study of peer processes in delinquent behavior.

> The old message that delinquency begins in the home is more disavowed than reaffirmed by our analysis. Insofar as it is present, it emerges in a new form. We firmly believe that need dispositions which are required by gang membership arise in the interactions between the lack of preparation for school-type achievement in the home and the absence of access to alternative adaptations to failure in the schools.

Our theory posits that delinquent behavior is a defense against the external realities that threaten a young person's self-esteem. Delinquent behavior is defensive in that it provides a way of avoiding, neutralizing, or counteracting situations which endanger self-esteem. At the same time, delinquent behavior offers experiences that promise a form of self-enhancement. The theory assumes that a derogated self-image is naturally aversive and that it will set in motion forces to dispel it. Delinquent behavior is interpreted as a manifestation of these forces.

However, not all delinquent behavior successfully defends against anxiety and a derogated self-image. Where high levels of anxiety and low self-esteem persist along with heavily delinquent behavior, we assume that the delinquency is serving some other function. The partial theory upon which this study is based does not fit this type of delinquent. We do not suppose that the approach of the kind of alternative school that we have described will be so effective with this type.

It is important to note that the theory as stated here primarily addresses the defense against the external threats which can arise from the performance-, regulation-, and evaluation-centered atmosphere of the traditional secondary school. Why the emphasis on the student role? No other role incumbent upon young people in our society is so fraught with failure as studenthood. William Glasser, in his book describing *Schools Without Failure* (1969, 26), has even asserted that "very few children come to school failures, none come labeled failures; *it is school and school alone which pins the label of failure on children.*"

To the extent that any role entails clear and pressing standards of achievement, it creates the conditions for success and failure. Achievement stands at the core of the student role. Constant testing, grading, and ranking are indicative of the salience of striving and of the built-in necessity of at least relative failure. Experiences of success and failure pervade scholastic life, especially at the secondary school level. In no other setting—at home, on the job, among friends—are the standards of achievement so clear and the means to attain them so narrow. The only adolescent role comparable in this respect to being a student is being an athlete; and today, the athlete role during adolescence is so closely tied to the schools as an institution that it may be said to be a role within it (Coleman 1961).

Note that we have not made a distinction between the sexes. The theory is intended to apply to adolescent boys as well as to adolescent girls. We have used the masculine gender in this report for convenience; it should be considered to be a neutral, general usage.

We make a distinction among delinquents, however; for not all delinquency is provoked by scholastic failure. Adolescents' self-esteem is affected by other experiences as well, experiences at home with their families, out on the street with their peers, and so on. Insofar as the source of provocation is not the school, then obviously a school-based program would not be expected to make a difference. We assume, however, that scholastic experiences are a major provocation for most heavily delinquent youth.

We suspect that these two distinctions are related. That is, the problems of heavily delinquent youth who are also highly anxious are probably not primarily scholastic problems. They are more likely to have their roots elsewhere, perhaps in the family. Whatever the specific cause or causes, these problems are manifested widely, in school and the community.

Provocation and Control

Two terms central to the theory are *provocations* and *controls*. By *provocations* we mean the experiences that motivate a person to be disruptive and delinquent. By *controls* we mean the goals and values that constrain a person from being disruptive and delinquent.

Provocation. The theory of delinquent behavior as a defense is linked to the concept of the schools as an institution through the following hypothesis: a major provocation for delinquent behavior is incompetence in the role of student. The youth falls short of his aspirations for scholastic achievement. Furthermore, he is likely to experience few if any other successes in school. He is not particularly popular or well known among classmates. He is unlikely to have many close friends at school and if he does, he is still isolated from the status structures of the school regardless of his peer relations. He does not excel in any extracurricular activities and he has no special interest or hobby in school at which he can demonstrate particular competence. The consequence of these experiences is a derogated self-image, a feeling that he is not worth much and never will be. Delinquent behavior, particularly disruptive behavior in school, is a defense against this self-derogation.

Such disruptive behavior consists of attacks on school property and personnel, including fellow students; theft; dealing in drugs; noisy, distracting, and insubordinate behavior; violation of rules about such behavior as smoking and movement within the school; and truancy. Disruptive behavior in school is especially appropriate as a way of coping with low self-esteem for several reasons. First, since the derogation is generated by scholastic experiences, the behavior occurs at the time and in the place where the pain is most acute. Second, the appreciative audience that enhances its effectiveness as a coping mechanism is more readily found at school than elsewhere. This last point deserves some elaboration.

Disruptive, delinquent behavior is conceived to be a public *performance*—a mode of self-presentation. It is hypothesized that such behavior is motivated by a desire to enhance the self by the approval of others. Disruptive behavior leads fairly easily to self-aggrandizement since it is not difficult to accomplish if one "has guts." In addition, the school creates a ready audience of peers with similar problems, who will not only observe and applaud but will often participate as well. And typically there is an undercurrent of adolescent negativity toward school even among those who would not behave badly themselves. This conjunction of elements at school makes it a likely stage for a disruptive, self-aggrandizing performance.

A third reason for coping by means of disruptive and delinquent behavior lies in the message it conveys. While functioning as a performance, the behavior is also a declaration of revolt against the criteria by which the person has come to regard himself as a failure. It defies the exercise of authority over both deportment and standards for scholastic achievement, devalues the devaluations, and rejects the devaluators (Cohen 1955).

Control. Not every youth who is failing as a student finds disruptive, delinquent behavior an appropriate way to rescue self-esteem. The element of control must be taken into account. Some youngsters are closely attached to people who would disapprove of such behavior, so much so that the approbation of disruption by a peer audience is offset. Where there are warm parent-adolescent relationships that might be ruptured, where there is love that might be withdrawn, where there are affectional, material, or other resources that might be withheld, disruptive behavior bears more costs than benefits and therefore is not displayed. This is the kind of restraining influence that Hirschi (1969) calls "social bonds." Many youngsters have too much "stake" in the social system to risk delinquent behavior.

When strong controls effectively counter strong provocations to be disruptive, then delinquency will not be a strategic defense against a derogated self-image. Unable to cope by engaging in disruptive and delinquent behavior, a heavily controlled youth may feel great anxiety or may take flight from reality, depending on his other coping skills and the other forces in his life. That is, alternatives to disruptive and delinquent behavior may be various forms of mental illness. Thus, the theory generates a hypothesis that the intensity (frequency and seriousness) of delinquent behavior will vary inversely with symptoms of mental illness, particularly pervasive anxiety among youth who experience role inadequacy such as scholastic failure.

Delinquent Behavior and Official Delinquency

The theory is meant to explain delinquent behavior, defined as the deliberate commission by a juvenile of an act he knows is a violation of the juvenile code which, if apprehended, may result in judicial response. Several implications of this definition should be made explicit. First, it is a *psychological* definition in the sense that it defines delinquent behavior from the point of view of the actor. Note that the behavior qualifies as delinquent only if it is "deliberate"—intended—and that the individual "knows" that it is in violation of the law. So, accidental and unwitting violations of a juvenile code do not qualify as delinquent behavior. For example, if a youth accidentally breaks a window, he or she is not a vandal. Although legal authorities may regard accidental or unwitting acts differently, our definition is designed to advance our understanding of individual behavior. For this reason, it may in some cases classify behavior differently than administrators of justice would.

The definition is psychological in still another respect. It specifies that the actor not only be aware of the violative nature of his act but also anticipate an institutional—"judicial"—response if he is caught. There are juvenile offenses whose commission is almost universally ignored by the authorities. For example, while it is against the law throughout most of the United States for minors to buy, possess, or use tobacco, minors are almost never detained or even warned about such behavior even when it comes to the attention of the police. Thus a judgment that behavior is delinquent takes into consideration not only the law but also its enforcement.

It should be clear that this definition of delinquent behavior does not ignore the law. It is a *social* psychological definition in the sense that it takes an individual's understanding of social norms into account. An act is delinquent even if the actor does not think it is wrong, so long as he knows it is against the law. Some young people believe that marijuana ought to be decriminalized. They regard it as unjust that using it makes them liable to legal sanction. But, since they know that they are so liable, their smoking pot is by definition delinquent. It may be that behaviors which violate laws believed to be unjust have different causes than other violations and are committed by different people and under different circumstances. If that were so, then perhaps we would need to change our definition to take this distinction into account. At present however, we do not believe it is necessary to do so: the correlates of marijuana usage, the clearest contemporary instance of controversial law, are pretty much the same as the correlates of consensually delinquent behavior, and they tend to be done by the same youth (Bachman et al. 1978; Gold and Reimer 1975).

It is important to recognize the distinction between delinquent behavior, as defined above, and *official delinquency*. Delinquent behavior refers to the actual incidence of delinquent acts in a given population (subject to the conditions just noted). Official delinquency refers to that small subset of delinquent behaviors whose perpetrators are apprehended by the police and recorded in the juvenile justice system's records. Official delinquency reflects not only the behavior of youth but also the behavior of the police and others in the juvenile justice system—the people who create the records. We are reporting a study of how certain kinds of schools might reduce delinquent behavior.

Because there is only a small relationship between delinquent behavior and official delinquency, schools might affect the former and not the latter. Indeed, it is altogether possible that schools could have opposite effects on them. An alternative school might reduce its students' delinquent behavior markedly. However, students might be stigmatized for attending "a special school for delinquents" by the police or the juvenile authorities. Because of that, or possibly because of their prior records, the youths may more likely be named official delinquents when they are caught at relatively minor offenses. More likely than this is that an alternative school program would actually affect its students' delinquent behavior and have no noticeable effect on their official delinquency because the official record is an insensitive gauge of delinquent behavior. The chances of getting caught for a chargeable offense are about three times in a hundred. Two out of three of the most delinquent 20 percent of American adolescents have no official records at all (Williams and Gold 1972). The official records do not mark the rise and fall of delinquent behavior in a community or for individual youth with any precision.

This distinction between delinquent behavior and official delinquency is important to keep in mind here, because while we collected the official records of the youth who participated in our study, we did not rely on them as a principal index of the effects of the alternative schools on delinquent behavior. We will later describe what we regard as superior ways to measure this. Meanwhile, we will use the terms *delinquent behavior* and *delinquency* interchangeably, as we have defined the former, and refer to *official delinquency* when we mean the records of the juvenile justice system.

A Promising Educational Program

Our theory of the etiology of delinquent behavior prompted our interest in a certain kind of alternative school. We hypothesized that there are two essential ingredients of alternative education that would determine its success at reducing disruptive and delinquent behavior: significant increase in the proportion of a youth's successful—versus unsuccessful—experiences, and a warm accepting relationship with one or more adults. Both of these pointed to the need for an individualized program.

We hypothesized that an effective alternative program tailors the educational process to the student in several ways.

1. The educational materials and tasks are appropriate to the student's present level of skills.
2. Their content appeals to the student's own interests.
3. The student is allowed to master them at his own pace.
4. Evaluation is based on individual progress—comparisons are made with the student's own previous performance, not with norms for age or grade.

Also characteristic of the alternative programs of interest is the suspension of the social norms that typically govern teacher-student role relationships. In their place are more informal, more personal relations. The differences between role relationships and personal relations have to do with their affective components and with the involvement of whole personalities in the relationship. Ordinarily, secondary school teachers are encouraged to assume a routine pleasantness toward their students that, in effect, amounts to affective neutrality. In the interest of fairness, teacher-student relationships are relatively constant from one student to another. Neither teachers nor students are supposed to take one another's peculiarities into account; rather, peculiarities must be submerged in the enactment of formal roles. Personal relations, in contrast, are affectively loaded and participants demonstrate their changing feelings toward one another. Each takes into account the other's individuality in their interactions, rather than holding the other strictly to the rules of a formal relationship. It is interesting to find this theme in William Glasser's account of a discussion he held with some tenth graders: "The discussion centered on how different the impersonal junior and senior high schools were from their recollection of a more personal elementary school. . . . the difference was very important to them" (1969, 217–18).

We hypothesized that in effective alternative programs, teachers would help create a unique relationship with each student. These relationships would be infused with a genuine liking and acceptance of the student but, on the other hand, would not conceal disapproval for some kinds of behavior.

By providing successful experiences and thus reducing the provocation of school failure, a program can break the etiological chain that is identified in the partial theory of delinquent behavior. The warm, accepting relationship with teachers also enhances the student's self-image. Furthermore, this kind of relationship is conducive to the formation of social bonds that strengthen the individual's controls over his behavior.

Such programs have already evolved, independently of any explicit theory. Anderson (1973) has shown that high schools in which students describe less exercise of bureaucratic authority and more informal, personal relationships with their teachers also create less student alienation from the school. One finds, in descriptions of alternative school programs for delinquent youths, emphasis on individualized curricula, ungraded classrooms, personal evaluation, and warm teacher-student relationships. A report on the Woodward Day School in Worcester, Massachusetts, is typical.

> Other programs [for aggressive and other emotionally disturbed children in the Worcester school system have] adopted many of the Woodward Day School features: a controlled small environment, location outside of public school walls, individualized attention, acceptance of deviant behavior, and an emphasis on improving the students' self image. (Kennedy et al. 1976, 721)

Swidler describes two alternative high schools in Berkeley, California, in similar terms.

> Group High and Ethnic High avoided teaching students about achievement, about success and failure. They concentrated instead on teaching students self-confidence and self-respect. The first element in increasing students' self-confidence was reduc-

ing the inequality of status between teachers and students. Casual, friendly relations between teachers and students lessened students' fear, and made the teachers seem approachable, nonintimidating friends. Students felt important precisely because, as one student put it, "The teachers were really friends with students." A second way to avoid evaluating students, and to build self-confidence, is to construct assignments with few possibilities for failure . . . . [At Group High] students were praised and rewarded for sharing their ideas with the group; not for having the right answers. Indeed, right or wrong answers, correct or incorrect facts and ideas, were subordinated to psychological and socio-emotional considerations. Students were not judged; they were encouraged to develop their individual potential. (1976, 220)

But in these alternative programs, as in other efforts to reduce delinquency, data are rarely collected to test either the effectiveness of the programs or their theoretical assumptions. One has to glean hints from the empirical literature on how separate components of the program might work if they were integrated.

Two studies are relevant here. In one, Joseph Massimo provided individualized counseling services to ten disruptive and delinquent boys, including the two components hypothesized to be present in an effective alternative school program: an increased ratio of success to failure experiences, and warm relationships with norm-abiding adults (Massimo and Shore 1963). Massimo made particular efforts to ensure that his clients were adequately prepared for the jobs they took, that they received guidance and assistance in keeping their jobs, and that remedial education was tailored to each boy's needs. Furthermore, personal support was available at all times, day and night, and Massimo maintained a flexible approach in his dealings with the boys. Follow-up studies demonstrated that the boys Massimo worked with became less delinquent compared to the control group (Shore and Massimo 1966, 1969, 1973, 1979). It should be recognized that while this was not a school program, it suggests elements of effective teacher behavior.

More directly pertinent perhaps is the Quincy, Illinois, alternative school program described by Bowman (1959). Sixty eighth graders who were performing poorly at their schoolwork were selected for study. Most of them were discipline problems at school and 41 percent had police or court records. Three groups of twenty youngsters each were defined randomly, two of these groups becoming special classes, the third continuing in the conventional junior high school program. The special classes differed in several ways from the traditional program. The students spent a larger share of their school day with one teacher who had volunteered to lead the class, who knew the students well, and who was sympathetic toward them. The children were not pushed to achieve; the pace was slow, tailored to their current levels of functioning.

> The efforts of the teachers were aimed at making school a pleasant experience; helping pupils learn the basic skills of reading, writing, and arithmetic; helping them learn the practical things they would use in their daily lives; and providing experiences in which they could find some success. (P. 59)

Clearly it was the intent of the program to maximize success experiences and provide warm teacher-student relationships.

The effects of the special classes were mixed but promising. The students in the alternative program showed neither more nor less gain in achievement scores than did the randomized controls. But their attitudes toward school improved along with their attendance, relative to the controls. About two years after the program began, official delinquency records were checked again; these revealed that the students in the alternative program had had fewer contacts with the police and that the offenses for which they were apprehended had become less serious. The control group was exhibiting the opposite trend. It is not clear from the published reports just what produced the positive changes. It appears not to have been real advances in scholastic abilities, although it seems likely that the students felt that they were making better progress, which psychologically may be more crucial than the objective fact. It also seems likely that social bonds with their teachers grew stronger and were thus able to provide some constraint against antisocial behavior.

The importance of warm personal relations with a socializing adult in the effective treatment of delinquents is underlined in a study by Persons and Pepinsky (1966). Eighty-two boys incarcerated in a state reformatory were selected as appropriate for a combination of group and individual psychotherapy. Half of them were randomly assigned to the treatment group. The authors write that

> one of the major objectives of every therapist was to encourage in each boy the development of warm, personal relationships,

both with the therapist and with the other boys in his group. (P. 330)

One of the more immediate effects of the therapeutic program was to raise the level of participants' scholastic performance in the reformatory school. Significantly more participants than controls made the scholastic honor roll. Another effect was improvement in the participants' behavior so that fewer of them were reported to be disciplinary problems and more were granted passes that permitted greater freedom at the institution (Persons 1967). Yet one might be skeptical about measures of effectiveness taken within the institution where personnel who make decisions are also aware of who is receiving treatment and who is not. More impressive are the differential records compiled by the randomized groups after they were released. After the same amount of time on the outside, 61 percent of the controls were reinstitutionalized compared with 32 percent of those treated.

It is plausible that any special effort would have some beneficial placebo effect—a phenomenon well known in social science and medicine. One explanation for this effect is that special efforts signal to the recipients that others care about their welfare, and this makes them feel better, work harder, and so on. Actually, this effect does not contradict the theory presented here inasmuch as we hypothesized that a prime ingredient of effective alternative schools is a demonstration on the part of teachers that they care particularly for their students. It should be noted that we hypothesize a particular sort of caring will be effective—one that minimizes formal role relationships between teachers and students—and we propose that at least perceived scholastic improvement is important too.

The literature on delinquency treatment programs shows quite clearly that many special efforts have failed to make noticeable differences. Different kinds of programs have been systematically evaluated—volunteer probation officers, various forms of group therapy, tutoring, and behavior modification to name a few—and they have not seemed to work (Gold and Petronio 1980). Especially relevant here is that one carefully researched alternative school program was not demonstrably effective. Reckless and Dinitz (1972) observed a program designed for seventh-grade boys who were nominated by their sixth-grade teachers as likely or possibly to get into difficulty with the law. Over the course of three successive years, 632 such boys were assigned to self-contained classrooms of 25 to 30 boys each, taught by selected and specially trained teachers. The classes met for three consecutive hours each school day and the students attended regular classes the rest of the day. The program differed from the conventional curriculum in several respects. The main thrust consisted of "role model" lessons in which positive behaviors in a wide variety of settings were presented, discussed, and practiced. Other features included: special efforts to improve the students' reading skills; the main disciplinary action was to send a student out of the room but not to the principal's office; the parents of students enrolled in the third year of the project were visited by the teachers; and the classes were composed of boys only.

The effectiveness of this program was assessed mainly by comparing the boys in the alternative program with a set of boys who were also nominated by the teachers as likely or possibly to get into difficulty with the law but were randomly selected to remain entirely in conventional classes instead. Reckless and Dinitz summarize the findings thus:

> On none of the outcome variables were the experimental subjects significantly different from the controls. This was especially and most painfully evident in the school-performance and police-contact data. There were no significant differences in the number of boys who experienced contact with the police, the frequency of such contact, or the seriousness of [self-reported delinquent] behavior. In regard to the school data, the dropout rate, attendance, grades, and school-achievement levels . . . were very much alike. (P. 153)

This summary was true both for data collected at the end of the boys' seventh-grade experience and three years later.

Apparently this alternative school program did not work. But, as we observed near the beginning of this introduction, alternative schools are not all the same and one should not expect the same results from them. It does not seem from Reckless and Dinitz's report that the Columbus, Ohio, programs that were observed put into operation the psychological processes that we have hypothesized would make an alternative school program effective. The boys' attitudes toward their teachers deteriorated over the school year, equally so among the alternative and conventional school students. It is notable that the reading skills of the alternative school students improved significantly compared to the controls; and that this improvement was reflected in a marked increase in these boys' confidence in their capacity to learn. But the conventional boys also gained some confidence over the year in their capacity to learn, so that progress on this score did not differentiate the two groups reliably. It seems to us that the emphasis given in the alternative program to a fairly fixed curriculum, frequent examination, and discipline by isolation probably worked against achieving warm, teacher-student relationships or a distinctive advantage over conventional programs in raising the confidence of the students in their scholastic potential.

It remained to be seen whether other alternative school programs that aimed to maximize the strength of certain psychological processes could actually put those processes to work and if they did, could be effective in raising the self-esteem of their students and reducing their delinquent and disruptive behavior. The following chapters review literature relevant to the theory; describe the programs that we found and how we went about testing the hypotheses derived from the theory; and report how and under what conditions the programs were effective.

Chapter 2

Theoretical and Empirical Background

The thinking that led us to a particular kind of school as a promising subject for theoretical and practical consideration did not spring full-blown from our imaginations. The problems with which we were concerned have concerned other social scientists for many years, and there is a rich research literature about them. Evidence relevant to the theoretical model that we began with can be found scattered throughout the social sciences. Since no one study provides data on all the elements of the theory, we drew upon the literature piecemeal. A review of the more pertinent sources will enable readers to put the present study in context. Readers will be able to judge to what degree the findings that we report later are credible because they are consistent (or inconsistent) with the results of other studies.

Our theoretical model, to recapitulate briefly, hypothesizes that many disruptive and delinquent adolescents behave that way because they are provoked by failure in school. Scholastic failure threatens to lower the youths' self-esteem. Under conditions of low social control, these young people turn to delinquent behavior to raise their self-esteem. This defense may be successful for enhancing their self-esteem at the level of conscious awareness, but it does not enhance their unconscious negative feelings about themselves, which continue to provoke their delinquency. It follows that, if these youngsters' experiences at school were altered sufficiently to raise their self-esteem at all levels of consciousness, their disruptive and delinquent behavior would subside.

However, this theory is not assumed to cover all heavily delinquent adolescents. Some, probably a minority nowadays, behave badly for other reasons besides being scholastic failures. Their self-esteem may be low for other reasons, in which case greater success at school would not reduce their misbehavior. Or their delinquency may have functions other than or in addition to defending them against threats to their self-esteem; in this case, raising their self-esteem would not ameliorate the problem. One way to identify these adolescents is by the characteristic that they are heavily delinquent despite their apparent success at school. Another way is that they have little conscious self-esteem despite persistent disruptive and delinquent behavior.

Scholastic Achievement and Self-Esteem

The first link in the hypothetical chain of our theory is that scholastic failure threatens adolescents' self-esteem. The preponderance of the data support this hypothesis. Studies employing various measures of both scholastic success and self-esteem have almost all demonstrated that better students tend to have higher self-esteem.

For example, Jerald Bachman (1970) tested this hypothesis among a representative sample of tenth-grade American boys. Self-esteem was measured at a conscious level, with a combination of items adapted from Morris Rosenberg's 1965 study and from Cobb, Brooks, Kasl, and Connelly's 1966 research. The measure included such items as "I take a positive attitude toward myself," "I feel I do not have much to be proud of," and "I am a useful guy to have around." Boys' responses correlated positively ($r = .23$) and statistically significantly ($p < .01$) with their reports of recent school grades.

Similarly, M. A. Prendergast and D. Binder (1975) obtained positive relationships using the Tennessee Self-Concept Scale, the Rosenberg Self-Esteem Scale, and the Houghton Mifflin Test of Academic Progress among 366 urban ninth graders. Edgar Epps (1969) found that scores on the Rosenberg measure of self-esteem were correlated with the scores of urban black high school students on the School and College Abilities Test or the Otis IQ Test, and with their recorded grades. Studies of upper elementary school pupils, which correlated the California Achievement Test with the Tennessee Self Concept Scale (Williams and Cole 1968), with Bills' Index of Adjustment (Bledsoe 1964), or with an adaptation of Stephenson's Q-sort measure of self-esteem (Bennett no date), all yielded positive correlations between self-esteem and scholastic achievement.

We have previously reported research (Gold and Mann 1972; Mann 1981) that demonstrates the relationship between scholastic achievement and self-esteem in ways particularly relevant to the present study. These studies measure self-esteem at unconscious levels with a projective test that will be described in some detail later since we employed it in this study as well. We have found modest but reliably positive relationships between unconscious self-esteem and grade point averages.

Geoffrey Maruyama and his colleagues (1981) have presented data that illuminate the background of the relationships between scholastic achievement and self-esteem. They have found that the social class of children's family at their birth and their scores at age seven on the Wechsler Intelligence Scale for Children independently and substantially relate positively to the children's self-esteem at age twelve. Both social class and IQ also relate to scores on various scholastic achievement tests taken at ages nine, twelve, and fifteen. Indeed, one can predict as well or better to twelve-year-olds' scores on the Coopersmith Self-Esteem Inventory from their family's social class at their birth and their IQ at age seven as from their current achievement test scores. Of course, social class, IQ, and achievement test scores are all predictive of children's graded performance in school—indeed, IQ and achievement tests were designed to do just that. So the relationship between scholastic performance and self-esteem does not originate in the secondary school. It is at least partly laid down much earlier. However, the grades that adolescents receive in junior and senior high school may further strengthen this relationship. Maruyama et al. speculate about this.

> Although our findings argue that self-esteem is directly affected by ability (and social class) rather than by past achievement, it may be that examination of different measures of achievement, such as classroom grades, would have yielded a different outcome. That is, even though grades may be a poorer measure of school learning than are standardized tests, grades seem more likely to influence self-esteem because they are a more salient benchmark of performance for children than are standardized test scores. Because children may never directly receive information about their performance on standardized tests, such performance may be less likely to influence self-esteem. Further, grades may share less variance with ability than do standardized tests, and therefore may be more likely to exert an independent influence on self-esteem. (P. 973)

A study by Edward Kifer (1975) lends credence to this speculation and confirms the developmental process. Kifer collected the cumulative school grades of second, fourth, sixth, and eighth grade students in a public school. He also administered the Coopersmith measure of self-esteem. Kifer found that students who consistently received the lowest grades since the second grade also expressed the lowest self-esteem, and that this tendency increased from the fourth through the seventh grades. However, the self-esteem of the poorest eighth grade students reversed this tendency: it was higher than the least successful seventh graders', although still lower than the self-esteem of the consistently best eighth grade students. Kifer offers two possible explanations for these findings which are not mutually exclusive. One is that scholastic performance has a cumulative effect, diverging the self-esteem of the most and least successful students. The other is that scholastic achievement becomes more salient with progress toward maturity, so that performance is more determinative of self-esteem in the later grades. Both of these interpretations are consistent with our theory. Especially interesting is the reversal of the trend at the eighth grade. We speculate that the invocation of defense mechanisms, particularly delinquent behavior, was buffering the impact of scholastic failure on the students' self-esteem.

Scholastic Achievement and Disruptive Behavior

One must be aware of the inadequacy of most of the data on the relationship between scholastic achievement and disruptive and delinquent behavior. Research on delinquency in the past and, for the most part, today as well, has relied on official records of apprehended, adjudicated, and sometimes incarcerated youths for indirect measures of the degree of delinquent behavior. But a relationship of official delinquency to scholastic achievement is built into the data by the process of creating the records, for it is more likely that an apprehended youth will acquire a record if an inquiry determines that he is doing poorly in school. Whether the actual commission of delinquent acts is related to scholastic achievement cannot, therefore, be conclusively demonstrated by official data. For this reason, we will review here studies that measure delinquent behavior by means of unofficial observation and self-reports.

John Feldhusen, John Thurston, and James Benning (1971) had third- and sixth-grade teachers in a semirural Wisconsin county nominate 2 boys and 2 girls in their classes who demonstrated exemplary behavior (e.g., "industrious," "productive") and an equal number who characteristically displayed disruptive behavior (e.g., "disrupts class," "bullies others," "tardy or absent without excuse"). A sample of 256 boys and girls was then randomly selected from each category for intensive study. The researchers found that disruptive pupils scored significantly lower in the reading and arithmetic sections of the Sequential Tests of Education Progress (STEP) than did the "good citizens," and that the difference between categories of nominees was greater at the sixth-grade than at the third-grade level. Follow-up studies five and eight years later by the same authors showed that the difference in scholastic achievement persisted through high school.

Carl Weinberg (1964) asked seventh- and eighth-grade teachers to identify the boys in their classes who (1) "contributed most to the solidarity of the classroom group by their outstanding efforts, excellent cooperation, demonstration of leadership abilities, and general all around willingness to help," or (2) "contributed most to the disunity or conflict present in the classroom through disobedience, lack of effort, and general nonconformity to school and classroom expectations." Teachers' nominations were checked with principals, vice-principals, office staff, and school records to assemble two categories of students who were clearly quite different in their reputations. Then students' STEP scores for reading, writing, and arithmetic were compared, and the disruptive boys' achievement was found to be markedly lower ($p < .001$). This was true among sons of both white-collar and blue-collar workers.

In sum, then, many studies employing different measures have established a correlation between disruptive or delinquent behavior and scholastic achievement. Of course, correlation is not causation; the relationship supports but does not confirm the hypothesis of a causal link between the two.

John Phillips and Delos Kelly (1979) have argued, however, that other data support the hypothesis that scholastic failure leads to delinquency rather than two alternative hypotheses: that delinquency leads to scholastic failure or that both delinquency and scholastic failure are correlated because they are each related to some third factor. "If school failure is indeed a cause of delinquency," Phillips and Kelly have asserted, "then any reduction in school failure (including leaving school, which would eliminate it) should produce a reduction in delinquent behavior among those individuals who leave. On the other hand, if delinquency somehow produces school failure . . . , leaving school should not affect delinquency" (p. 199). They then cite studies reported by Delbert Elliott (1966) and Elliott and Harlan Voss (1974), both of which demonstrate that boys' delinquent behavior declined after they dropped out of school. In some respects, these data are strong support, because we might have expected that school dropouts would become more delinquent. For one thing, a theory emphasizing social control would predict that the severance of bonds to a socializing social institution would weaken social control and increase delinquent behavior. Second, the proverb that "the Devil finds work for idle hands" implies that school dropouts would have lots more time to be delinquent—and they are also under less adult surveillance. Phillips and Kelly conclude that scholastic failure seems to provoke delinquent behavior, not so much because of its long-range implications for success in our society but rather because of the current distress that it arouses. They write, "[W]e view delinquent behavior as a way of coping with social stigma and loss of self-esteem associated with failure" (p. 204).

The idea that scholastic failure causes disruptive and delinquent behavior would be more certainly confirmed by an experiment in which scholastic achievement is raised and disruptive, delinquent behavior subsequently declines.

Self-Esteem and Delinquent Behavior

In a previous study, we made a distinction in the concept of self-esteem that is especially relevant to the hypothesis of delinquency as a psychological defense (Gold and Mann 1972). Measures were taken of both conscious and unconscious levels of self-esteem. (We will describe these measures later.) Among eighth-grade boys from a lower-class, rural Michigan junior high school, no significant difference in conscious self-esteem was found between highly delinquent low achievers and high achievers who were seldom if ever delinquent; but there was a difference ($p < .10$) between the high achievers and low achieving boys who were *not* highly delinquent. On the other hand, the low achievers who were highly delinquent registered the lowest *unconscious* self-esteem, significantly different from that of the high achievers ($p < .002$). These data were interpreted to mean that delinquent behavior served a defensive function, elevating the boys' conscious but not their unconscious level of self-esteem.

Mann (1981) has replicated this finding among fifteen- through eighteen-year-old boys representative of all the boys in that age group residing in the contiguous forty-eight states. Fifteen- to eighteen-year-old boys whose unconscious self-esteem was markedly lower than their conscious self-esteem also confessed to significantly more delinquent acts than did other boys. This was not true, however, among younger adolescent boys. Similar results with the same measures have been obtained by Sidney Berman (1976) and by Michael O. Miller (1980).

The previously mentioned study by Massimo and Shore (1963) points to the causal relationship between self-esteem and delinquent behavior. Twenty fifteen- to seventeen-year-old boys were identified by their histories of antisocial behavior, repeated truancy, chronic problems of school adjustment, failing grades, aggressive acts, and reputations with attendance officers, courts, or police; and they were at the point of leaving school, voluntarily or involuntarily. Ten boys were selected at random from these twenty and offered the services of a clinician from the Judge Baker Child Guidance Clinic, primarily to help them find employment. They received comprehensive services for ten months, while the other ten boys did not. At the end of that time, only three of the ten boys in treatment had been placed on juvenile probation, compared with seven of the control group ($p < .10$).

To measure self-esteem in this study, Shore, a clinical psychologist, rated pairs of stories elicited by Thematic Apperception Test pictures. Five stories were told at the beginning and five at the end of treatment. The ratings were done in a triple-blind design, the rater not knowing which story was the first one of a pair, which boys told which pairs of stories, or which pairs were told by the same person. Improvement in self-esteem was observed more frequently among the boys in treatment than among the untreated group ($p < .01$). Its causal relationship to changes in delinquent behavior is suggested by the authors: "The authors indicate that the first area of change is in attitude toward self." It is also notable that the Metropolitan Achievement Test scores of the boys in treatment improved in reading, vocabulary, and arithmetic, while the scores of the control boys declined ($p < .01$). This occurred even though no special attempt was made to get the boys in treatment back into school or to tutor them.

A follow-up study testified to the importance of self-esteem in the change process.

> Of great interest is that comparison of the follow-up stories with those given immediately after treatment indicated the same course of change as in the before and after treatment comparisons. That is, self image changed most, control of aggression next, and attitude toward authority least. No boy showed a change in control of aggression who had not first

changed in self image, and no changes were shown in attitude toward authority unless there were changes in the other two areas. (Shore and Massimo 1966, 612)

Howard D. Kaplan (1980) has reported a predictive study that also links low self-esteem to delinquent and disruptive behavior causally. Over four thousand junior high school students were asked on a questionnaire about their attitudes toward themselves (e.g., "On the whole, I am satisfied with myself" and "I feel I do not have much to be proud of") and about their deviant behavior in the previous year (e.g., "Sold narcotic drugs," "Cheated on exams"). These data were collected twice, about a year apart. For each of the twenty-two deviant acts in the questionnaire, Kaplan identified those students who had denied ever doing that act up to the first administration; he divided these students into those who had reported high, medium, and low self-esteem. Then he compared their later reports of deviant acts. As hypothesized, for each of the twenty-two acts, more of those who had given evidence of low self-esteem at the start of the year reported having committed the act during the ensuing year than did those who had indicated high self-esteem. Apparently, low self-esteem was a precondition for delinquency.

Florence R. Rosenberg and Morris Rosenberg (1978) also tested the sequential relationship between self-esteem and delinquent behavior, using the longitudinal data collected by Bachman (1972). They found that

[t]he weight of evidence is in the direction of Kaplan's speculations. For the sample as a whole, and for the lower and higher socioeconomic classes separately, the analysis of cross-lagged panel correlations suggests that self-esteem has a stronger effect on delinquency than delinquency has on self-esteem. And this is especially true in the lower class where the social support for such activity may be stronger and the social condemnation weaker. For the same reason, delinquency appears to damage the self-esteem of the higher SES youngsters more than of the lower SES boys. (P. 289)

Finally, Elliot Aronson and David Mettee (1968) demonstrated experimentally how low self-esteem can generate delinquency. The researchers created differential levels of self-esteem among women enrolled in an introductory psychology course by giving them randomly predetermined reports of their profiles on a personality test they had just taken. A subject was told either that her profile indicated that she has "a stable personality and is not given to pronounced mood fluctuations of excitement or depression" or that her profile showed that she has "a rather unstable personality and is given to . . ." Following this experimental induction, the women participated in a blackjack game, during which an apparently malfunctioning card-dealing apparatus gave them what they thought was a covert opportunity to cheat. Significantly more women cheated whose self-esteem was threatened ($p < .03$).

Thus, several studies support the hypothesis that low self-esteem leads to delinquent behavior.

Types of Delinquent Youth

Those who have studied the problem of delinquency or have tried to do something about it typically observe that delinquent youth are not all of a piece. Of course, each individual is unique. But more than that, there are apparently crucial differences in the reasons for youngsters' disruptive and delinquent behavior and in the ways that they misbehave. One conclusion from this observation is that no prevention or treatment program is likely to reach all heavily delinquent youngsters.

In an effort to understand delinquency better and as an attempt to tailor intervention efforts more suitably, researchers have for a long time been trying to formulate a verified and useful typology. (For reviews of this literature, see Ferdinand 1966, and Gold and Petronio 1980). Some typologies are based on the nature of the delinquent acts (e.g., personal versus property offenders); others, on the structure or dynamics of the offenders' personalities (e.g., characterological, neurotic, and psychotic); and still others, on the social conditions under which the offenders live (e.g., lower class versus middle class). Empirical studies have not been kind to the typological schemes; support for any particular typology has been inconsistent at best.

The typology that seems to have the most solid empirical support at this time is Lester E. Hewitt and Richard Jenkin's (1947) distinction between socialized and unsocialized-neurotic delinquents. Gold and Petronio have summarized the findings.

One must be cautious about some of these data because the procedures for sorting adolescent offenders into these classes relies on clinical judgments of unknown reliability; there is a large proportion of "mixed" types (Shinohara and Jenkins 1967, Jenkins 1968); and the claims for construct validity of this classification system often rest on relationships to variables, such as broken homes or parent-child relationships that were known to and probably considered by the clinical classifiers. On the other hand, Shinohara and Jenkins (1967) found different MMPI profiles for incarcerated boys of the two types, the unsocialized type scoring higher on indexes of psychopathology. Randolph, Richardson, and Johnson (1961) compared social and solitary delinquent boys on a correctional "ranch" and also found the MMPI profiles of the latter—solitariness is a hallmark of the unsocialized delinquent—showing more disturbance. Quay (1964) found Hewitt and Jenkins' (1946) types by factor analyzing probation officers' ratings based on information in the case histories of incarcerated boys. (1980, p. 510)

It seemed to us that the distinction between socialized and unsocialized-neurotic delinquents was relevant to our theory of delinquency. As we pointed out earlier, we believe that our theory covers most adequately those youth whose disruptive and delinquent behavior is an effective defense against threats to their self-esteem. We supposed that the effectiveness of the defense would be evident in the relative lack of anxiety and depression felt by the youth. If delinquency was not an effective defense, the theory predicts that young people would turn to other means to ameliorate their low self-esteem or they would experience mental disturbance. If heavily delinquent youth were also anxious and depressed, this would indicate that either they were among those for whom delinquency was not an effective defense and would therefore soon behave differently; or that they were of a type whose delinquency was generated by different forces not covered by the theory. In either case, they would be identified in Hewitt and Jenkin's typology as unsocialized-neurotic. An alternative school program would not have much effect on this type: their disruptive and delinquent behavior might decline whether or not they participated in an alternative program as they found other defenses; or their misbehavior would persist because schooling was irrelevant to its origins.

Obviously the theory is not presently very satisfactory for research on anxious and depressed adolescents, because it cannot predict whether they will be highly delinquent or hardly delinquent at all. But suppose it is assumed that most heavily delinquent youngsters are, at least under contemporary American conditions, of the socialized type. Thus it follows from the theory that, in general, the more delinquent youth will be less anxious, and that this will be true especially if one considers only school failures. There are some data indicating that this is so.

John Davies and Rodney Maliphant (1971) asked teachers at a boys' boarding school in England to nominate "refractory" students; they then identified thirty named by at least two-thirds of the teachers. Thirty boys who were never so nominated were matched with the refractory boys for age and form (grade) in school. To measure anxiety the researchers relied on base heart rate and changes in heart rate with the introduction of stress conditions. They found that the refractory boys had lower base heart rates and that their heart rates were less reactive to the threat of shock for error or overlong delay in a reaction-time task. Davies and Maliphant replicated the finding of less reactivity in another sample, comparing seven boys attending a public secondary school whom teachers rated as unresponsive to punishment, hostile to authority, dishonest, aggressive, indifferent to adult approval, and generally bad, with seven boys whom teachers rated in contrasting terms.

Ray Naar (1964) has contributed evidence measuring anxiety based on experts' ratings of the House-Tree-Person (H-T-P) drawing test. His delinquent group was composed of thirty boys fourteen to sixteen years old, incarcerated in a correctional institution in Virginia; thirty nondelinquent boys were selected from an urban public school in an area with a high official delinquency rate, matched with the delinquents in age and tested intelligence. Both of the judges who independently and blindly rated anxiety levels from the H-T-P found *fewer* signs of anxiety (excessive, irrelevant detail; hesitant, faint lines; shading) in the *delinquents'* drawings.

One of the series of studies by Milton Shore and Joseph Massimo (Shore, Massimo, Mack, and Malasky 1968) is informative on the relationship between delinquency and anxiety. They report that TAT stories told by the boys who received the experimental services contained markedly more signs of guilt at the end of treatment than did those told by the control group. Furthermore, increases in measured guilt were reliably and positively correlated with improvement in Metropolitan Achievement Scores. However, both the level of guilt and its correlation with achievement subsided in the years after treatment was terminated. If one can equate signs of guilt in this study with general anxiety, the results suggest that effective treatment induces both scholastic improvement and, by disallowing an established delinquent pattern, higher levels of anxiety. However, as the provocation to delinquency declines—the effect on self-esteem of more successful scholastic performance, steady employment, and so forth—anxiety declines. The results further suggest that one risk of only partially effective treatment is that anxiety will continue to grow in the absence of an effective delinquent solution, perhaps to a degree that generates pathology. Indeed, one of the ten treated boys had to be hospitalized as a psychotic, while none of the control boys entered a mental institution (Massimo and Shore 1963).

With delinquency and anxiety measured in different ways in each of these studies, the youths defined as delinquent proved to be in some sense less anxious. We know of no studies with an opposite finding. While this pattern of evidence seems supportive of the theory, we remain cautious on this point because the theory is itself ambiguous about the unsocialized-neurotic delinquent. The important point to be made here is that there is reason to suppose that highly anxious and depressed students who are referred to an alternative school because of their disruptive and delinquent behavior may not respond so well to the program as the less anxious and depressed students will.

Chapter 3

The Schools

We have presented a partial theory of delinquent behavior that conceptualizes delinquency as a psychological defense against a derogated self-image. The theory identifies failure in the role of student as a major threat to the self-image. Thus, it implicates the schools as a significant provoker of delinquent behavior. Concomitantly, the schools are recognized as having great potential for reducing delinquency. Elements of a type of educational program have been described that might effectively draw upon the school's potential.

In order to test this theory and to assess the practical effects of the kind of schools the theory points to, it was necessary to identify educational programs that actualized the theory and enlist them in research. We decided not to set up our own alternative schools, tailored to meet research needs, for several reasons. First, we are not trained to do so and would have had to call upon others to operate the school in any case. But, more important, we wanted for practical reasons to study such programs in their natural settings, rather than as a more artificial, special, and perhaps temporary experiment. It seemed likely to us that the results of our research would be more credible to makers of educational policy if they were established under normal conditions. Furthermore, we realized that programs seldom operate at their full potential when they begin; it takes a while for everyone to learn the ropes in what nautical people call a "shakedown cruise." So we hoped to save years of waiting by identifying appropriate programs that had already passed through this initial phase and were performing satisfactorily according to those responsible for them. Finally, we hoped to find a variety of programs to study, schools that were significantly different from one another except that they shared what the theory proposes are the essential elements for effectiveness. Such a combination of differences and commonalities would provide a better test of the theory and a more convincing practical demonstration. We judged that these were reasons enough to sacrifice the kind of control we may have exercised over our own program.

Our search for suitable alternative schools was guided by the following criteria: (1) most, if not all, of the school's students must be disruptive and delinquent youngsters who would otherwise be excluded from school; (2) the program must clearly incorporate the two hypothetically essential elements of an effective program—students must experience a preponderance of successful scholastic experiences by means such as individualized curricula and grades based on progress and there must be substantial suspension of the conventional teacher-student role relationship so that teachers could provide warm, personal social support to each student; (3) the program must have been in operation long enough that the people responsible for it were satisfied with it and expected it to continue largely as it was for the foreseeable future; and (4) the program had to be oversubscribed, so that there would be eligible students who could not attend and would comprise an ample comparison group and the assignment of students to the alternative schools or the comparison group from the pool of eligible students could be done at random.

The search actually began years before this study as Gold became involved in workshops on delinquent youth. These workshops often included educators responsible in some capacity for alternative school programs for disruptive adolescents. The workshops led to discussions with the staffs of alternative school programs, and eventually a file of ongoing programs was created. Part of the personal network that developed included the founders of the Michigan Association for Educational Options. Its list of members was an important source of candidate programs.

Initial contacts were made with administrators of several dozen alternative programs to determine which ones would be appropriate for and interested in the study. About a dozen programs survived this initial screening. The others turned out to be already defunct or to have doubtful futures, largely because of financial problems; or they were serving all the eligible students; or they served very few disruptive or delinquent students; etc. Visits to the surviving programs accomplished two purposes: further information was gained about the orientation of the programs as well as about the willingness of the staffs to collaborate in a research project; and leads were provided to other alternative programs that seemed to meet the criteria.

Finally, five programs were identified that seemed to have suitable characteristics. They deliberately served a substantial number of disruptive and delinquent students. While their programs differed, their philosophies and operations stressed the development of warm, personal teacher-student relationships and experiences of scholastic success. They had more referrals than they could accommodate and were willing to cooperate in making the surplus accessible to research. Their staffs, from the teachers up to the district administrators (and, in one case, the school board) endorsed the research effort. The programs seemed stable; they had been in operation for at least two years and were likely to continue for the foreseeable future.

As it turned out, one of the five programs did not last through the following year. One of the things we learned early on in this study and which we were continually reminded of throughout, is that alternative schools are particularly fragile, especially those devoted to troublesome adolescents. Their staffs work under considerable stress, not the least of which is opposition from within their own school system and in their community. It does not take much to close such schools—an incident of violent behavior, an unfavorable report on achievement test scores, a tight school budget—any of these will do it. As we will report, the fragility of these programs creates special problems for studying them.

Another of the five programs proved, upon closer, systematic observation, not to meet our selection criteria.

The reader's understanding of the kind of alternative school that we were looking for may be enriched by descriptions of what actually happened in each of the schools on one of the days that we visited it.

Alpha: "All Loving People . . ."

Alpha occupied one wing of an elementary school building. It was a red brick, one-story building located in a suburban neighborhood. It was surrounded by parking lots on what were once the school's playgrounds. At the time, signs out front pointed the way to the different entrances to the several departments then housed there, such as the Instructional Materials Center and Alpha.

> The Alpha doors are apparently locked when we arrive shortly before 8:00 A.M. because a girl, who we suppose is a student, pushes it open as we approach. She asks, "Alpha?" We tell her who we are, and she welcomes us. She waves her hand toward the dim, wide corridor, "This is it."
> Alpha occupies several rooms on both sides of the corridor. At one end on the right is what we learn later to be the workshop room. The

blackboard testifies that it was once a classroom. Now it holds only a few tables and a variety of wooden chairs arranged in a loose circle. A connecting door leads to a set of small toilets and beyond these, to a large, almost empty room that must be the teachers' office. It contains three large desks and a few beat-up files. Across the corridor is the students' lounge, an old refrigerator, ragged upholstered chairs and couches, magazine racks stuffed with paperbacks, tables with a coffee maker and accessories, and a radio. The blackboard slate hardly shows from beneath a haphazard collage of cutout faces of rock stars, TV personalities, and other teen world "Faves." The walls bear dittoed notices and have more decorations. One colorful brown paper poster reads:

A	L	P	H	A
l	o	e	a	l
l	v	o	v	p
	i	p	e	h
	n	l		a
	g	e		

Mike, a teacher, is bustling around the office gathering materials when we arrive. The kids who have arrived are in the lounge, drinking coffee and juice, talking, looking at the day's newspaper. John, the other teacher, and Shirley, the aide, arrive about 8:10 A.M. Mike calls to the students and they cross the hall to the workshop room, drawing their chairs into a tighter circle. The students have steno pads—their journals. They are dressed variously but nothing they wear is particularly weird or conservative. One boy, who is actually balding, wears his shirt open to his waist and no undershirt.

The session begins with a "public interview." The kids get a chance to find out who we visitors are by asking questions. We are told that we can "pass" a question. Mike is conducting this workshop and leads off the questioning. Meanwhile, a few kids drift in and take chairs, and the circle is widened to draw them in. We learn later of the rule that after ten minutes into the workshop, latecomers must wait in the lounge for the break and they lose some credits for the day. The first part of the workshop, before the break, is spent talking with us about the study we are planning. At the break, most kids go back to the lounge. The staff goes into their office.

After the break, the workshop becomes a group therapy session, not unprecedented, John tells us later, but not typical either. Julie has not been at Alpha in over a month, and she did not attend regularly before that. The group is discussing whether Julie will be allowed to remain in Alpha. It is a tense discussion. Julie cries. The kids press questions about her absence and what she was doing. Two girls tell about their running away from home. Some kids want to stop the discussion, but most want to continue it. Mike has a "quiz" he has planned to give the kids but they never get to it. At 9:30 A.M., the session ends. Mike says that he and John will decide about Julie. The kids start to move out. They drop their steno pad journals into a cardboard box. We didn't see anyone writing in the journals during the discussion.

The kids disappear from the building very quickly but at John's insistence, Julie stays for a conference with him and Mike in the lounge. The second workshop kids have not arrived yet. The three of them are alone. Shirley gets coffee for everyone, and we gulp it down before the second workshop starts.

As they come in, many, but not all whom we ask, of the second workshop kids agree to let us read their journals. They are quite different from one another and from day to day. They consist mostly of reactions to each day's session. This is supposed to be the primary content, but Mike says that the entries drift away from that, and the kids have to be reminded to record their reactions. Kids also write messages to Mike and John about their personal problems; comment on things that have happened outside of Alpha, like books they've read or films they've seen; enter answers to exercises done in the workshop; tell jokes and draw pictures. Some pictures border on pornography. Each day John and Mike read the journals and write comments in them—encouraging, elaborating on the kids' observations, and sharing their own feelings. They may suggest a conference about something. They do not grade them or correct spelling or grammar. Mike and John do this every afternoon, when the second workshop has gone. The kids may *not* look at each other's journals and they trust each other not to.

The second workshop also begins with a "public interview." After the break, John continues to lead the workshop with a lot of participation by Mike, unlike John's one comment in the first workshop. The workshop is on a film they'd seen about adults' views of teenagers. Then John reads aloud a series of thirty-six questions from a newspaper supplement on "How well do you know your parents?" (e.g., "What color is your father's eyes?") Kids record answers in their journals. Mike remarks to us that this is a more typical workshop activity than the first group's therapy session. It will be followed up tomorrow.

Afterward, Mike and John make some phone calls and they settle down at their desks to read journals. Mike says he uses the journals to suggest topics for the workshops because the kids sometimes tell him in their journals about things they won't bring up in the discussion. Afternoons will also be spent in conferences with the kids. Each kid meets with a teacher at least once a month. At these times, kids and teachers will write "contracts" for individual projects for credit or they will review kids' progress. Current contracts include learning to play a guitar (one boy demonstrated in yesterday's workshop), making a skirt, and learning karate (also a recent workshop demonstration).

Beta: ". . . Is Better"

Beta was also housed in a wing of an unused elementary school. From the outside, it looked very much like the Alpha building. Out in the parking lot there was a sign that seemed hostile to us: "Beta Staff and Student Parking by Permit Only." Inside, the layout of rooms, though somewhat smaller, was also similar to Alpha's.

The rooms have been decorated by the kids—a few ecology and peace posters on the walls, and mobiles hanging from the ceiling, each signed by the kid who made it. Slogans and poems are written on the window glass ("Beta is Better"; "It was long ago and far away, the world was much different than today. And all the good things came for free to all the kids . . . like me. . . .") Also taped up are student progress charts and previous seminar notes.

At 8:00 A.M., when school seems to start throughout this district, the kids are already in the large room, a former classroom, in the middle of the three-room unit. The staff room is on one side, meeting/classroom on the other. A portable radio in the lounge is tuned to a rock and roll station. Coffee is available to all in the staff room; the kids help themselves. Several of the students are barefooted.

At about 8:15 A.M., the first seminar group seat themselves in the meeting room around an enclosed rectangle of tables. Students have found their looseleaf notebooks on a bookshelf and have placed them open before them on the table. Dean begins the session. Audrey, the other teacher, arrives seconds later and one of the girls greets her—"Here's Mom!" Audrey tells about the car trouble she's had and, in conclusion, places her hand on a girl's shoulder and says "That is my excuse." Audrey does not notice, but the girl seems hurt. She whispers to the girl next to her, "What did she mean by that? I wasn't late."

A few more kids come in as the discussion about the Beta picnic proceeds. No one takes notice of their entrance. The newcomers take their notebooks and find a place around the tables. Later one of the tardy boys describes the trouble he had with his car—a loose gas cap caused gas to slosh on his fender.

The teachers are seldom addressed directly during the discussion, but when they are, it is as "Dean" and "Audrey."

Dean leads the first session of the day although Audrey feels free to enter the discussion and even redirects the process. The seminar is about the forthcoming picnic, making plans, hearing reports of work groups. The kids must decide on food, how to get a lot of Betas to come, how to eliminate pot and alcohol, and activities. They try to follow a problem-solving sequence that is posted on the wall.

Audrey whispers to us that this discussion is atypical, much more loose than usual. Ordinarily, the seminar runs an exercise that is more structured.

The looseleaf notebooks contain the kids' contracts, along with feedback (progress) charts for each; and the scoresheets for participation in seminar. Kids get points for using seven communication skills (e.g., expressing feelings, restating someone's contribution). They score themselves as the discussion goes on. Later, they get Dean or Audrey to initial their scores. Laura and Pat show me their notebooks—Laura has no progress charts; Pat's are carefully drawn and up to date. The points mean credits toward graduation and so the kids—most of them—keep track of theirs. Besides the points they get in using the communication skills, students get extra points for writing out their contributions on a form provided for this purpose. Each student has planned a week in advance for how many points he/she wants to earn that week—in contracts and seminars. There is some concern today that the picnic on Friday will interfere with their plans since it is not point making. They discuss how to build points into the picnic (e.g., by going, being on time, etc.).

One of the communication skills is to be open about feelings. They are practicing a phrase, "I feel attacked when . . . you criticize me as you just did, etc." and they earn points for saying it at appropriate times. They may also earn points for saying "I feel good when . . ." Some of them try to say these things as often as they can, and they get laughed at.

Kids contract for various kinds of activities: reading books; a project on local/state government including interviews with the mayor, council members, police chief and legislators; making a skirt (a girl wore hers to seminar today); lifting weights. Before seminar, during break, and after, Audrey and Dean urge kids by name to complete projects. One boy is unlikely to finish any of his, and he does not say anything in seminar today either, hardly opening his notebook. Audrey says later that she thinks he is just marking time this year, unsure of what he wants to do but wants to "be in school." Audrey also assures us that few kids hand in unsatisfactory projects; more often, they simply will not hand in any. A few kids—Audrey wishes there were more—earn almost all credits with contracts and almost none in seminars. Most active discussants are also consistent contract completers.

While talking to Laura about her notebook, it becomes clear to us that the Betas are required to be both participants and observers of their own participation in discussion, that is, to be in "two places" at once. Laura calls this a "Beta-thing" or "Beta-way." But she says that while the observer part is not carried outside of Beta, the communication skills are. Kids don't tally up their scores at home, although they relate to their parents with the skills they've learned. (Laura's father is an instructor, so Laura may carry more out of Beta than others.) While discussing all the self-sufficiency, participant observation, and organization required of Betas, Laura says that "Some people think that the Betas are dummies, but actually you've got to be smart."

Patrick decided to enroll in Beta after taking a psychology course at his high school that was taught in Beta way by a former Beta teacher. Pat had dropped out of school and found when he came back that he could tolerate school taught in this way. Pat also takes courses at the high school in order to make up for the time he lost. He elects as many independent studies that he can. He is having trouble completing his reading contract, although he is ahead on his math and work contracts. He's trying to read *The Lord of the Rings* trilogy and keeps falling asleep. After the seminar, Pat shows his progress charts to Audrey. She notes how far behind he is and suggests a conference about it for the next day, suggesting that different books may be a solution.

L. High: "We Try to Recognize . . . Real Achievement"

We also visited the conventional high school that Pat attended. It is a big school, quite modern and equipped with chemistry, biology, and physics laboratories, gymnasium, pool, audiovisual accessories, and what seems like every technical support educators might need. The hallways are broad, the floors sparkle, and some areas are air-conditioned. It is apparent from various posters near the entrance that this is not just a school but a community resource, used by other community groups as well as by other schools.

We arrive at about 7:40. A sign in the parking lot says that we must register our car at the office in order not to get a ticket.

There are students waiting outside near the various entrances and in the vast cafeteria. After registering the car, we are directed to the office of one of the three vice-principals. Ms. M. apologizes for not having already prepared a schedule for us, but she says that she's been tied up the last few days with the Honors Convocation that was held the night before. She recalls that we want to visit classes from which Beta students are drawn. That means for Ms. M. that we should see classes with students with low motivation, who have experienced lots of failure, and who take as few academic courses as they can. She begins to talk, perhaps in contrast, about the Honors ceremony; she and the other administrators and counselors all wore academic robes, and there was an academic procession. Ms. M. tells us that the school district has received a federal grant to expand their advanced placement program; the grant will permit 40 percent more students and a few more selected teachers to take part.

For the first hour, we are scheduled into the individualized reading class. We learn that the class developed as a response to students' requests to their counselors that there be a class in which they could get credit for reading what *they* want to read. There are about 25 students in the class, sitting at rows of tables facing the front of the room. A study hall teacher is substituting for the first few minutes for Mr. L. whose car had a flat on the way to work. The students are reading many different kinds of books; hardbacks, paperbacks, textbooks, workbooks. Some are doing their homework from other classes. One boy in the front row is sleeping with his head on his arms. The room is fairly still, with only some quiet whispering.

After a few minutes, Mr. L. arrives and the substitute leaves. Mr. L. glances about the room and goes to his desk. We introduce ourselves. Mr. L. tells us about his system: Each student keeps a daily record of pages read and comments on the content and writes a book report in accordance with a structured form that Mr. L. shows us. The students are graded from "A" to "E" with 90 percent of the grade based on the reading rate. The students either choose their books from the Instructional Materials Center or they buy them.

During the class, two people come in to see Mr. L. in his capacity as advisor of the yearbook. One gives him a camera and flash attachment, which Mr. L. puts in an unlocked file drawer as the class looks on. He asks if the seniors have gotten their appointment cards for senior pictures. This generates movement to the teacher's desk—appointment cards, hall passes, book report forms. Mr. L. takes attendance. When the talking gets loud or continues for an extended time, Mr. L. gives the students a long hard look and they stop. At about 8:45 one boy fills out his daily report form and turns to some homework. By 8:50 most of the others begin to fill out forms. Mr. L. announces that two of the students in the class won Honors at last night's ceremony, one in Family Life and the other as Best Woman Athlete.

The talk gets louder. Many students rise and move toward the door. At the bell, they leave. Mr. L. tells us that he likes having this class first hour: he has only a few administrative things to do and some control functions, so he gets a lot of other work done.

Second hour: We visit Mr. S.'s clay class, but no one is working in clay today because pieces are being fired. Mr. S. tells us that he will have the students sketch and anticipates that they won't like it. Yesterday he took them outside to sketch, but he has been told by the principal that he can't do that anymore because the other students will want to.

The room fills up quickly. The kids sit in groups of two to five around bare tables, chatting. We notice that every group but one is unisexual. One boy is sitting with three girls. There are twenty-two students. Mr. S. gets their attention by calling out "Listen now, you bandits . . ." They banter with him about how "hot" it is in the room, but they do not object much and get quickly absorbed in the sketching assignment: to draw an object "they love" as though it were melting or emanating light. He remarks that he got the idea from a student in another class yesterday. One of the boys in this class knows who: "That's Skip's work," he says and holds up a stunning crayon drawing which was lying on a side counter. Mr. S. tells the class that he will not grade them "punitively" for this assignment. Later, he repeats that he won't use the grades "as a punishment."

During the class, two kids drop in to talk casually with Mr. S. and some students in the class. Mr. S. goes down the hall with one of these visitors. The class continues to work as before while he's gone. One of the boys is eating chips out of a paper bag; a girl offers Oreo cookies around.

When Mr. S. returns, he announces that the Art Club is holding a car wash to raise money. He asks for volunteers but gets none. Then he calls out hopefully to specific kids. One of the boys asks Mr. S. if he will treat for breakfast. Mr. S. answers that, if they make a lot of money, he'd buy everyone lunch. Jim volunteers, and Mr. S. tries to get the girls to volunteer because "Jim is going to be there," and there's some laughter. Then Mr. S. goes from table to table with a pad soliciting volunteers. Students feel free to refuse even when asked at such close range.

Now we can see a girl talking to Mr. S. in his office adjacent to the studio. As they talk, Mr. S. smiles and grasps the girl's outstretched hand.

At 9:40, Mr. S. instructs the students to put their names on their work. They begin to file up to deposit their drawings in a large portfolio that Mr. S. has opened on the counter near the door. The bell has not rung but some of the students go out into the hall. Mr. S. goes out and asks them what they are doing. One says that they are looking at the art exhibition in the showcase there. Two of the pieces are the work of a boy in this class: clay figures of bloody and torn body parts. A boy asks Mr. S. if he can go to his locker. Mr. S. says "No." Now Mr. S. tells those outside to come in but only some do. The rest congregate just outside the door with Mr. S. Two students are still sketching at their tables, and they stop only when the bell rings and the class disperses.

Third hour: We visit the class on the "Pre-School Child." It is held in a suite of three rooms—a carpeted colorful playroom, a classroom, and a large multiple kitchen with several stoves, sink, refrigerators, tables, and chairs. In the playroom are a few high school girls and nine small children, variously playing with toys, pitching pennies against a wall, and preparing to do some painting. Ms. J., a small woman in white tennis shoes, tells us that these are mostly children from the neighborhood. They attend from Tuesday through Thursday. This is the last day of these children's session so, Ms. J. tells us, they are especially excited.

All of the students in the course are girls. Usually some work with the children while others observe particular children, writing "evaluations" according to an outline on the blackboard in the classroom. Today, several girls are writing reports or reading a child development textbook in the classroom. The classroom routine is not normal today. It being the last day for the children, the students do not have to write plans for subsequent days or read as much. They will all participate in the festivities instead, with milk and a decorated cake. The students in the classroom are now casually talking among themselves, some about the children. One girl comes in protesting with a laugh that "little Eddie" wiped his paint-laden hands on her pants. In mock despair, she displays the stains. Ms. J. is also in the classroom at this moment—she's been circulating constantly—and remarks that people have to be careful of what they say to Eddie; he gets ideas for mischief easily. Ms. J. tells us that she teaches the class more formally on Mondays and Fridays, reviewing the past week and planning the one coming up. Ms. J. also complains to us that the girls, who are supposed to be writing reports and making plans for the next session, are not able to take responsibility for their own work and are idle a lot.

As the end of the hour nears, those girls who do not have direct responsibility for the children today gather at the door that leads from the playroom out into the corridor. The girls who are working with the children remain until the next shift comes in, then they leave too. Only a few of the children even seem to notice that there has been a change.

Fourth hour: Mr. K.'s basic geometry class. Ms. M. has warned us that these are not "top geometry students." Mr. K. tells us that it is a good class. He has put letters and numbers on the blackboard, which coordinate numerical averages with letter grades. A boy comes in, studies the numbers, and exclaims that he "missed an A by one point!" As students seat themselves, Mr. K. gives them cards that summarize each student's grades so far. He announces that he will discuss the exam and grades tomorrow. The students copy over their grades and pass the cards up to the front, where Mr. K. collects them.

The lesson begins, Mr. K. goes over the answers to yesterday's problems. The students ask questions ad lib. Then Mr. K. assigns the next set of problems from the textbook and the class goes to work. There is some talking among the students, and some movement to the pencil sharpener and from desk to desk. The students are free to help one another or to ask Mr. K. for help. When they finish, they go to Mr. K.'s desk to check their answer against a key. Mr. K. moves about the room.

A boy rises from his seat with his geometry workbook rolled up, to get a fly that's been buzzing around the room. Mr. K. warns him not to step on the wrestling mats that are piled in the back of his room. The class pays little attention to the boy's efforts. He stalks the fly and seems to be seeking attention and laughs. Finally, Mr. K. tells him to settle down, and he goes back to his seat.

A girl is staring into space with her forearm resting across the top of her head. Mr. K. goes over to her and asks "Is that a hand?" meaning "Are you asking for some help?" She teases him: "Yes," she says, holding out her hand, "that's a hand." Mr. K. says "Oh" and moves on.

Now many of the students are visiting with one another. One goes up to the front to check the answer key, then sits in Mr. K.'s chair with a broad smile on his face. Mr. K. notices him and joins in the role switch: he sits at his desk and asks him to read off the answers to the problems. As the student does so, Mr. K. instructs him to go more slowly. The boy is obviously enjoying himself and the class is razzing him. Later, Mr. K. tells us that this razzing is common and that he too is sometimes a target. The students talk quietly to one another and Mr. K. When the bell rings, the students file out.

We watch one of the shifts having lunch. There are actually two large cafeterias, one for hot food, one for fast food. Three "lunch aides"—middle-aged women—monitor each cafeteria and one male teacher moves between the rooms. We tell the aides what we are doing there. One of them tells us that "Beta is for students who are supposed to go to school but don't want to." She is not sure that Beta is still operating.

Students sit where they like; they may go outside to smoke in designated areas.

We are invited to have lunch with the assistant principal in a conference room off the main office. Lunch is served by the commercial foods students and their teacher. Mr. B. tells us why he thinks the enrollment at Beta has declined: the program is no longer new; there are now more classes at the conventional school; and parents have discovered how unstructured Beta is. He says that Beta is a program in which kids can remain formally enrolled but still not actually go to school regularly, with neither parents nor the school finding out.

After lunch, Ms. M. takes us to see the display cases in the main hall. She points out that the displays honor students for accomplishments that are not recognized by the Honors ceremony. She says, "We try to recognize any sort of real achievement—anything that is above average."

Fifth hour: Mr. L.'s American Government class. As we arrive, a few students are gathered around the teacher at his desk. We introduce ourselves and sit in the back of the room. Twenty-two students are in class today.

Class begins with a test. The students work silently. Two need pencils, so they sign them out from Mr. L. by putting their names in a prearranged spot on the blackboard. One boy signs his name "X." Mr. L. remarks dryly that he "will know who that is." Not a sound except pencils on paper, a cough, shifting feet. After about twenty minutes, some students finish and deposit their test papers—question sheets and a mark-sense card—on the front table. In return, they pick up another dittoed sheet of homework, which they begin immediately. Mr. L. begins to circulate among those still working on the test but there is no exchange between them.

Mr. L. borrows a pocket calculator from a girl in order to figure the grade point average for a boy who was absent yesterday when he went over averages with the rest of the class. Mr. L. comes to the back of the room and tells us that this is a good class—he means well-behaved—even though it meets in the last hour.

The students are moving about the room now talking to one another, mostly about the homework. As the talking grows louder, one of the students calls Mr. L.'s attention out loud to an error in the homework assignment. After checking it over, Mr. L. announces a correction and some students groan. Mr. L. also points out that the answers to the two questions overlap and a girl says challengingly that they are exactly the same. Mr. L. corrects her and begins to talk about the answers. No one seems to listen except one boy who enters into a dialogue with him. Mr. L. tells a boy to leave another boy alone who is still working on the test. A few students are grumbling, half aloud, about the ambiguity of the homework assignment.

The hour is drawing to a close and one boy has put away his books and sits with an unlit cigarette in his mouth and a lighter in his hand. The bell rings and the room empties quickly.

Another teacher comes to the door and asks Mr. L. where "the meeting" is. Mr. L. excuses himself to go out into the hall which is almost empty already.

ACE: ". . . Like a Family"

When we first became acquainted with the ACE alternative classroom, it was located in the school/administration building of what had been a large denominational orphanage. Only two of the cottages that were scattered under the trees of the campus were still residences. The others now housed various social services, as did other floors and wings of the main building. On the floor below ACE, classes were held for the school districts' emotionally impaired elementary school pupils, whom we later overheard the ACE kids refer to as "the nuts." By the time we began our research, ACE had been moved from this campus to the ubiquitous empty elementary school building elsewhere in the school district.

We arrive at ACE at about 8:10 A.M. The ACE secretary is bustling about. She offers us some coffee along with the morning newspaper. We stroll the corridor looking at the bulletin boards and posters.

Rod, one of the teachers, arrives. He wonders out loud whether to show a film called "Runaway Railroad," which he got from a ninth-grade teacher in one of the conventional schools. It seems too juvenile for the ACE kids, but he'd like to show a film. It's getting toward the end of the term and he and the kids need a rest.

The students begin to arrive at about 8:25 A.M. They greet their teacher by his first name. Most of them deposit their schoolbooks in the classroom and go down to the basement. When Linda, the other teacher arrives, she and Rod and we go downstairs too, to a lunch-room. We do not sit with the kids who are drinking coffee and smoking around a large table, but join other adults at a staff table, a designation left over from the orphanage days. The conversations at the two tables are quite the same—baseball and TV programs and such.

When it is time to begin the school day, Rod calls across the lunch-room to the kids. They respond immediately and we go upstairs again to the ACE wing: three offices off a corridor, at the end of which is the classroom. The classroom looks typical: blackboards, rows of student armdesks, bookshelves, cabinets, and so on. But there are two large teachers' desks up front, and a floor-to-ceiling partition is folded against the back wall.

Linda talks with the students as they settle in about how she slept all the day before and got two hits in last evening's softball game. We are introduced as "not being from the FBI or the CIA and not here to sniff out dope." Linda then begins a discussion of a forthcoming ACE picnic. One boy asks her to call his mother to confirm that ACE is going on an outing and that he'll need some pocket money, because he "needs proof" to get money.

It is time to start class. The partition is drawn, dividing the room in halves. Rod tells us quietly that the division is mostly by reading ability—above/below sixth grade. The upper group will spend most of the time in discussion, the lower, on workbooks. We sit with the lower group, taught this morning by Rod.

Rod passes out workbooks on fractions to the eight boys and one girl in the group. He has graded their work, he announces, and he puts letter grades and their numerical equivalents on the blackboard. Thea, a dark-haired, obese girl dressed in jeans and a light wind-breaker, sits in a corner by the blackboard where she obviously cannot see the figures Rod is writing and does not move. But she says nothing. Rod reads the letter grades "so far"; the kids are to turn the grades into numbers according to the table on the blackboard and figure their grade point averages. Most of the grades that Rod reads are A's and B's, with a few C's and one D. Rod tells us later that the grades are based on effort as well as quality; that they are higher than the same work would get in high school; and that the work is at a lower level, too. Thea remains dissociated from what is going on. Rod goes over to show her the equivalent values and helps her to figure her average.

Then Rod introduces a new subject to the whole group: how many digits indicate tens, hundreds, thousands, etc. The boys are attentive, but Thea still seems somewhere else. Rod tests whether the students understand the lesson by reading numbers aloud while the students write them on half sheets of ruled pages he has passed out. Everyone then passes his answer sheet to the person to the right for the purpose of grading them. The boy to the right of Thea asks Rod how to grade an answer if it is crossed out, as Thea's first two are. Rod says, "Mark them wrong." Rod and the boy exchange knowing looks.

We note already that ACE is more academic than Alpha or Beta. In less than one hour, there has been more testing and discussion of grades than we heard all day at the other two programs. When we share these observations later, Linda says that ACE is expected to do a lot of teaching. While its students do take classes at the high school, they earn many of their credits at ACE.

At about 9:40, Leonard comes in from his early class at the high school. He hands another boy a pack of cigarettes as he passes him and settles with a deep sigh in a seat by the blackboard. He sits for only a few minutes, then goes out again. The numbers lesson has gone on without anyone acknowledging Leonard's coming or going. Rod is teasing the class with numbers now: he is reading large numbers too quickly for them to write them down and asking them where the commas go. Most can't keep up and object. Jokingly Rod says, "You should have learned this in the fourth and fifth grade."

Near 10:00 A.M. there is a break. The students engage in horseplay, like dueling with pencils. Some go to the toilet off the corridor. The whole room empties except for Thea, who remains in her seat, staring down at her practice workbook.

The partition is folded back at the break. It is Independent Study time for everyone: art projects, history, mathematics, etc. The students pick up workbooks, folders, project materials. One boy takes over one of the teacher's desks, clearing it for his drafting project. All the students are told to stay in the room because, while it is crowded this way, the staff is exercising closer control now than usual. It is near the end of the term, Linda says, the students need to finish their projects, and they tend to wander more if allowed to work elsewhere, like in the lunchroom or the corridor. Gary, an aide, joins Linda and Rod in the room, and the three circulate, helping kids focus, urging them to concentrate on their projects, answering questions, and providing materials. During this activity, the biggest boy in the class comes up behind Linda and covers her eyes. Linda smiles, takes his hands away, and suggests that he get to work on his project.

Linda goes out into the corridor where Ron, the ACE administrator, is standing. She tells him that she thinks one of the boys is stoned. She briefs him: the boy has missed seventeen days of school so far; is arguing that he should get his credits if he does all his work, despite his absences; the family is litigious. Ron agrees to speak with the boy and calls him out of the classroom. They go to Ron's office.

Two of the boys in the classroom are punching each other on the arm. One of them keeps an eye on Linda to see if she is watching. If any of the staff sees this, no one says or does anything. The discipline has been low-key. The staff depends a lot on distracting the kids, changing activities, quiet suggestions. In one instance of chronic fooling around by Sheri, who often seems to attract boys' attention by attacking them (writing on their shoes, pushing them), Linda tells her to change her seat and work elsewhere.

During Independent Study, some students leave for classes at the high school or for work. Those who work part-time earn fewer credits.

After Independent Study, Linda asks the group if they want to see the film. She explains that it might be juvenile; and she tells them that if they decide in the middle of the showing that they don't want to see the rest of it, they should say so, not fool around by throwing pencils and stuff at the screen. They voice vote to see the film this afternoon.

Social Studies: The partition is drawn again. Linda sorts the kids into their groups. Rod takes the upper group now, although it is not exactly like it was earlier. The unit is on "psychology" and each student has a folder containing materials he has collected. Rod passes out a dittoed test—matching phrases to definitions. It is on psychoanalytic terms: e.g., "ego" = "the self," "reaction to a threat" = "ego defense mechanism." The students work at it diligently. One of them is sitting at the teacher's desk while Rod is perched on an armchair. When they are finished, the kids pass their papers to their left for grading. Rod reads the correct answers out loud and discovers that there is some mistake in his key. He straightens out the confusion.

It is lunchtime and the kids are excused. They leave their papers with Rod as they go and deposit their psychology folders in a cardboard box. Rod tells us that he and the other staff would rather not give grades, would be happier with a "pass/fail" system, but that it is not possible because of the pressures that ACE gets from the schools to which the students will return next year. As it is, Rod says teachers question the high grades that students earn at ACE since they do low-quality work at the conventional school afterward.

The aide presides over the lunchroom. Rod and Linda go out for lunch. A pair of kids pick up a hot lunch at a small window, some have brought their own, many go without any lunch at all. As before, the kids sit separately from staff, talking, smoking, and now listening to a radio someone has brought. Gary takes a vote on whether the group wants to spend the physical education time outside or in the gym this afternoon. They voice vote for outside. After about forty-five minutes, Gary announces that it is time for class again, reminds the kids to clean up and to push their chairs in under the tables. They do so and move along upstairs.

In the classroom, Linda announces that Ted will be graduating with the high school class at Ford Auditorium next week. Ted blushes. Linda jokes that they should all go to the ceremony with an ACE banner and party whistles. Rod whispers to us that Ted had been expelled from the high school for possession of marijuana. He has kept up by going to ACE and taking two night school classes. Ted is one of ACE's "successes."

Class has not formally convened yet, but some kids have returned to their independent study projects. Others are playing chess or three-dimensional tic-tac-toe.

The movie is shown. Only two-thirds of the morning's complement are present; the rest have gone off to conventional classes or to work. Those present watch quietly. Two fall asleep on their arms. Rod remarks as the shades go up again that they haven't had an easy day like this for quite a while.

After the movie, the class moves to the gym for volleyball. Linda has told them that the playground is infested with wasps and they trust her judgment to overturn their earlier vote to go out. Rod appoints two boys to choose up sides. Ron and Thea watch. Linda and Rod also play. The kids don't play well, but they seem to enjoy it and stay organized throughout with little staff input.

ACE must vacate the gym for another group. They all return to the classroom for the twenty minutes before the day ends. Nothing is planned and things get a little flaky; a tall, lantern-jawed boy whom the others call "Reverend Smith" takes a Bible from a bookshelf and standing before the class, begins to read, "And the Lord spake to Moses thus, saying. . . ." Linda interrupts him, reminding him that he's been spoken to before about this. She talks about the separation of Church and State and ends up by saying that Bible reading bothers some people. The boy puts the Bible back on the shelf, but he continues to talk to a few classmates near him about the verse. "And the Lord spoke to Moses, thus saying . . ." he repeats. Then he says several times, "Isn't that a lovely verse?"

Other conversations are going on. The two boys are punching each other's arms again. Lara is giggling. Linda gets everyone's attention by demonstrating how to hypnotize a chicken. Then a student goes out into the corridor and makes a face through the glass in the classroom door. Linda immediately turns this into a game: anyone who can look through the window for ten seconds without cracking a smile can go home early. A few kids take turns going outside while the rest, including the staff, make faces from the inside. This goes on amidst hysterical laughter until it is time to go home. No one gets to leave early.

As he gathers up material, Rod says that he is afraid that teacher layoffs will kill the ACE program. Teachers with seniority who want to keep *some* job will replace him and Linda, but they will not be right. Then the word will get around and students will stop coming to ACE. He says "ACE is like a family." Next year the program moves to a school building to save rental money at the campus. Rod is concerned because it is likely to be more restrictive there, "Like there will be no place for the kids to smoke."

R. T. High: "Sprint to the Finish"

The high school from which the ACE students were referred is a two-story wide-windowed red brick building situated in a suburb of Detroit. The school is in the midst of modest, single-detached homes. The grounds are cramped, given over almost entirely to parking areas. When we arrived at about 7:40 A.M., the parking areas were quite full, many cars were parked along the surrounding streets, and the roads were heavy with yellow school buses.

Students are waiting in clusters all around the school, some are already going in the various entrances. We go in right away, too. Students fill the corridors. Most are standing at their open lockers, but some are chattering around tables in the large cafeteria. There are a few staff members at cafeteria tables doing some kind of paperwork with students in line. This scene in the cafeteria reminds us of the ACE students waiting in their lunchroom for school to start, except that there is no coffee here and no one is smoking.

At 7:48 A.M. a signal bell rings. From outside, from the cafeteria, from doors all over, lines of students form and begin to move densely through the corridors in orderly two-way traffic. We notice one couple necking as they walk, another girl has placed her hand deep into her boy friends' back pocket. One boy is grinning and carrying a white mouse on his shoulder; another, similarly grinning, carries a juvenile raccoon in the same way; and a teacher who is monitoring the corridor outside his room replies to our wonder that today the graduating seniors are permitted to take their tamed animals out of the biology laboratory. This is the last day of classes for the graduating seniors; most of them take final exams next week.

A woman teacher comes out of the cafeteria and is met by a girl who hands her a gift. The teacher says "How nice! I know—you want to pass the course." They both laugh. The teacher says, "You're sweet" and puts her arm around the girl's shoulders as they walk down the hallway and around the corner. Another bell signals the start of class and suddenly the corridors are almost empty.

But soon students appear in the hallway again. They all carry passes to somewhere, most of them to the Media Center (the library).

The principal, Dr. S.—we are corrected by the secretary when we ask for Mr. S.—can give us some attention now that he has finished an urgent meeting with a staff member. He takes us to the head of the English department and calls her out of her first class. He explains who we are and tells her that we should visit B classes because ACE students are most likely to have gone to those. Ms. I. invites us to her class while she does some things with her students. Then, she says, we will go over the schedule and pick classes. Her first-hour class is a graduating class in the A track. She warns us that the seniors will be "squirrelly" today, and Ms. I. is afraid that the class will be "chaos."

As we walk in, the room falls silent; everyone is in a seat and the seats are all lined up in the usual rows. We are introduced briefly and sit in the back of the room. Ms. I. returns to her desk, where she has been going over individuals' folders, checking them for completeness so that she can assign final grades. The students put their folders in order at their desks and then bring them to the front of the room. Ms. I. has enlisted a girl to help her check the folders; this girl sits at the teacher's desk while Ms. I. stands behind it. Students whose folders have already been checked or who are waiting for Ms. I. to be free to check theirs move freely about the room talking quietly with one another. A boy asks, "Can we go out in the hall?" Ms. I. replies, "Not if you want to graduate." The boy chuckles. Ms. I. is obviously joking; she means simply, "No." There is no further discussion of it. The student clerk has a question for Ms. I., who is chatting with a boy whose folder the clerk now has; the girl grabs Ms. I.'s arm to get her attention. A girl and a boy are engaged in some physical horseplay at the front of the room, only a few feet from their teacher. She ignores them and soon they stop. After all the folders have been checked, many students bring Ms. I. their yearbooks. She seems to be a popular teacher. She writes in their books and they write in hers. At 8:50 A.M., the class files out for the second hour. Ms. I. wishes them luck, and she reminds them that only those students who have missed more than three class sessions during the term must take the final exam in that subject.

Second hour: Mr. B.'s "B" English class. "B" is for "Basic"—for students who are reading significantly below their age norms, are often absent, are marginal students generally. The B classes are smaller, with fewer than twenty students whenever possible. Mr. B.'s second-hour class has eleven boys and four girls. Today is a spelling lesson. Mr. B. goes over a list of words on the blackboard: *through, though, thought, quit, quiet, quite.* He is interrupted by announcements over the intercom. This happens in second hour every day, because this is the first hour that all the students are in school. For optimum use of buses, the students come for first or second hour and stay for fifth or sixth hour.

After announcements are broadcast, there is a special feature in recognition of this last day of senior classes; a senior girl sings a folklike song, accompanying herself on a guitar. It is a nostalgic "remember" song, about "the times of your life." Afterward, Mr. B. resumes the lesson without comment.

He is going to administer a test now and erases the words on the board. A boy jokingly asks him to leave the words there and Mr. B. jokes back, "As it says in Scripture, 'The Lord giveth and the Lord taketh away.'" The students converse quietly from seat to seat as Mr. B. passes out paper. They fall silent as he calls their attention to the test. He reads about thirty words to them, illustrating each in a sentence, and they write. After all the words have been read, some ask for words to be repeated, and Mr. B. repeats them. Then the students pass their papers forward to the teacher's desk. Some of the kids ask Mr. B. for passes—they want to go to their lockers to get some materials to study for another class and to go to the end-of-term informal talent sessions being held in the music room. He gives a pass to everyone who asks. He wishes them a good weekend as they leave. He gives the rest dittoed worksheets with "Word Search" exercises. Mr. B. holds up his yearbook and invites "Anyone who has a good word to say can write in my yearbook." No one accepts his invitation. These students do not appear to have yearbooks.

While they work at various things or do nothing at their desks, Mr. B. tells us about B students. They are more likely to be absent than other students, although this whole class was here this hour. B students, he says, are not so highly motivated. They have poor family and social backgrounds. Many drop out.

One of the boys in this class is a recent arrival from Lebanon. He has asked Mr. B. if he might ask us about getting into college. Mr. B. calls him over to where we are sitting, introduces us and leaves us, to work at the front desk on the papers that have been turned in. The Lebanese boy is an atypical B-track student: he is here to learn English better and he is expected to move into the A track in a year or so.

Third hour: "Tip" S.'s American history B class. The usual routine is followed today: the students read aloud in turn the paragraphs Mr. S. assigns to them from their textbook. Today's lesson is about Cuba,

Castro, the Bay of Pigs, and the late sixties in general. The recitations skip from page to page but always forward. The students read laboriously. (Mr. S. explains later that it is his main object to get these students to read as much as possible because they need the practice badly.) He corrects their mistakes, and he throws out questions about the meaning of words and the significance of the events. Students call out answers ad lib, and a few do most of the talking.

There is some commotion in the hall just outside the door. Mr. S. simply closes the door against the noise. A student remarks loudly that "You are not acting like yourself today." Mr. S. explains that the seniors are expected "to create some tension and conflict today." Another student observes that one of those seniors is Mr. S.'s son. Mr. S. ignores the comment and goes on with the lesson. Three students have their heads on their desks and are not following the reading. Mr. S. calls on one of them, who finds the assigned paragraph and the others become alert. Mr. S. reminds a student that he has an appointment somewhere now and excuses him. Then the teacher reviews some of the words again and passes out a dittoed quiz on the material they have just read. We notice that the questions and the vocabulary words are the ones that Mr. S. paid special attention to earlier. The exam is open-book, and Mr. S. tells us that this is a further effort to get these students to read.

As the students work on the quiz, Mr. S. circulates, helping one student with a question, encouraging others. The boy to our left is not taking the quiz; he has folded it away in his closed textbook. Mr. S. talks quietly to him; we hear him urge the boy "to sprint to the finish." The boy tells his teacher that, because he just missed his second-hour class, he will not graduate anyway. One of the assistant principals has put him "on report." The students who hear this commiserate with their classmate, and one urges him to "appeal." Since the student is doing this term over, we learn from Mr. S. later, this situation is especially disturbing to him. As Mr. S. circulates away, the boy begins to work on the quiz.

Others are finished now, and they take their papers to the front of the room to check their answers. Ms. S. tells us that these kids in the "B" track need instant feedback. After checking their answers against the key and marking them with red pens, the students deposit their papers in folders in a cardboard box on the teacher's desk.

Mr. S. keeps the students at their work and fairly quiet. After talking with one girl, he pats her a few times on the top of her head. Mr. S. approaches the troubled boy again, urging him to take the quiz, and the boy tells him that he has finished it. (But he has not gone to check his answers.) He explains to Mr. S. that he missed his second-hour class "doing Mr. R. a favor," namely, taking a boy home because he was "bombed." Mr. S. says that that boy had been in his first-hour class, and he was all right then. But, Mr. S. supposes, that student has a drinking problem and might have been drinking in between first and second hour. He suggests that the boy speak to Mr. R. about the matter. Then the student goes to check his answers.

In the minutes remaining before class ends, the students and Mr. S. banter. One of the boys remarks that he's going to try to get into Mr. S.'s class again next term. Mr. S. pretends dismay and asks him if he wouldn't rather hear Mr. M. lecture next term. The boy says he doesn't like to listen to lectures; he'd even rather have Mr. S.'s quizzes every day.

Fourth hour: Mr. M.'s American history "B" class. We have been told by the history department head that Mr. M. doesn't like visitors and that we are welcome only in the prelunch half of the class, which straddles the lunch hour. But Mr. M. greets us cordially in the hall. He explains that the class hour is split around the lunchtime, that he will lecture during the first half and give a quiz after lunch. He doesn't think that we'd care to watch his students take the quiz.

Mr. M. begins by making some announcements about next week's schedule for this class and takes attendance intently while the students talk among themselves. Then the teacher begins to lecture from behind a tabletop lectern on his desk. As he talks, the students take notes and occasionally raise their hands to ask questions. Mr. M. calls on them almost immediately and by name. He does not stay at the lectern long. As he warms to his topic, he leaves his desk to move up to the first row of students. He is telling what it was like on the home front in Detroit during World War II—rationing, war production, victory gardens. One of the boys begins to interrupt frequently with wisecracks. Finally, Mr. M. asks him to stop it; "Give me a break," Mr. M. says and pats him on the shoulder. The boy quiets down for a while but begins again a bit later and is ignored. Mr. M. finishes his remarks before the bell rings and says so. The students gather their materials and some move toward the door, heeding Mr. M.'s instructions not to go out in the hall. One boy suddenly grabs Mr. M. in a wrestling hold around his middle. Mr. M. smiles, says in mock panic, "Don't do that! Don't do that!" and the boy lets go. Soon the bell rings and they all leave.

The students eat their lunches in the cafeteria where they have a choice of sandwiches, a hot meal, or a salad bar. They may sit where they like, and they may go into the gym or into some corridor areas in the central wing. But, since lunch is in two shifts and classes are always in progress, they may not go into most corridors. Teachers are on special assignment today by those corridor doors, wary of the seniors acting up. Rock music is playing over the cafeteria sound system.

There is a faculty lounge off the cafeteria, but only a few faculty members are there today. We eat lunch with Mr. B. and Mr. S.; they escort us through some of the special facilities—the Media Center, the music room. There are a few students in each. In the Media Center, some students are reading newspapers, others are sitting and talking. A small group of students are meeting around a table with a teacher. In the music room, a pair of students are fooling around the piano, playing pop duets. The music teacher is eating his lunch at his desk and talking to his accompanist and a student. He rises to tell us that his program has been rated "superior" for several years running now and points out that the walls are crowded with framed awards. As we pass to the fifth-hour class, we notice that there are a few students working individually in the metal and electronic shops.

Fifth hour: Ms. C's "B" English class. As we walk into this room, one of the boys recognizes us from Mr. S.'s history class. He asks if we are "surveying the Basic classes." We answer that we are visiting "different kinds of classes." There are eleven boys and two girls in this class; Ms. C. says that a few students are absent today. She tells us that about 60 percent of this class's sessions are spent in individual reading, and today is one of those days. The class is reading a paperback novel about big-city gangs, *The Outsiders*. Ms. C. announces that, to be on schedule, students should be reading chapter ten today. Some kids have already finished the book, some are way behind. Students are reading this book, another book or magazines, or they are talking quietly with their neighbors. Ms. C. circulates. She asks one student, who has finished *The Outsiders*, if he would "do something for me"; she wants him to read a book she is thinking of using next year and give his opinion about it. The boy hesitates. Another boy calls out to volunteer, and Ms. C. gives him the book and tells him something about it. She asks another boy how he's coming on his report and where his book is today.

We are struck by the similarity between the way Ms. C. runs this class and the "independent study" sessions at ACE. While the work in this class is limited to reading, the teacher's function seems to be the same, the atmosphere is similarly relaxed, and the students' activity varies from doing nothing to forging ahead. When Ms. C. asks a girl if she has anything to do, the girl answers "Yeah, talk." Ms. C. shakes her head disapprovingly but says no more and moves on. This girl and a boy will spend the whole hour talking, and at one point, the girl massages the boy's shoulders. Some students have taken off their shoes.

Right outside the window, one can see some boys—probably seniors—tossing a frisbee. First one student in the class, then others go to the window to watch. Ms. C. is passing back worksheets, acrostics taken from a scholastic magazine. Each student's work is different. Some students deposit theirs in their folders in the cardboard box at the teacher's desk; one boy crumples his up and throws it in the wastebasket.

A boy announces that he has finished *The Outsiders* and asks if there is another book available by the same author. Ms. C. says "No." and she suggests that he look in the drawer for another book. He goes to a drawer and rummages through it. He takes out Salinger's *Franny and Zooey*. "*Franny and Zooey?* What's this about?" Ms. C. touts him off it: "That one is sort of hard to get into. There's a lot of philosophy in it." She helps him to find another book.

Apparently one of the boys at the window has not finished *The Outsiders,* so Ms. C. tells him to go back to his desk and read. The boy returns to his desk, remarking to the boy behind him that he'd better read too because they have to finish the book today. But neither read; they sit and talk instead.

Another student asks the boy who has just taken a book from the drawer if it is any good. He says "It's all right. It ends better than it starts." "Any rumbles?" "One fight—at the beginning." "Any chicks?" "Yeah. Some." Ms. C. asks the boy if he's going to serve out his detention time after class today. "Not today." he says. "OK." says Ms. C. Ms. C. tells us that students have a week from the day that they come late to class to make up the time. The bell rings and the students leave. Next week, Ms. C. tells us, she will quiz them on *The Outsiders,* using study questions that she passed out earlier. It is also a writing exercise, she says. We are quite tired and decide not to stay for sixth hour. We have been told that the extracurricular activities that usually meet at sixth hour are over for the term and only a few sixth-hour classes are in session.

Before we leave, we hunt up the principal to thank him for his and everyone's cooperation. We find him going into Ms. I.'s room. He says that he has to listen to some appeals.

Evening Youth Program:
". . . Quite Businesslike

For reasons which will shortly become apparent, we will describe the fourth alternative only briefly. The Evening Youth Program (EYP) was quite different from the preceding three alternative programs. It was large, with capacity for 400 high school students. While it started each term nearly full, we discovered that there was a substantial attrition rate.

EYP operated from 5 to 9:15 P.M. Monday through Thursday. It was a structured program. Its students generally took four classes, two of which were traditional vocational training. The remaining subjects were either English, social studies, or math. Each class met for two hours each night for two nights each week. The program had thirty teachers and an auxiliary staff of ten—counselors, reading specialists, the administrator, a psychologist, and a social worker. With the exception of the administrator, all of the teachers and staff were either moonlighting or had been laid off from other jobs.

As we enter the school—the program is housed in a junior high building—we notice a uniformed police officer inside, near the door. (He is present throughout the evening.) The halls are bustling with students. The bell rings and they quickly disappear into classrooms. Before classes begin and during the fifteen-minute class change break, only a few students stop into the library, which seems to be the ad hoc counseling center.

The school is quite businesslike. Teachers vary in their approaches, but in general follow a traditional pedagogy modified to include considerable seatwork. The curriculum is a truncated version of the district's usual regimen.

The teachers circulate, working briefly with individual students. Students are graded on their progress. We find the cohesiveness and "sense of mission" of the other alternative programs absent here. Teachers are generally in traditional roles. Students are also in the more traditional roles to a large extent.

Students are referred to the program because of chronic discipline problems, poor attendance, and failing grades. The program administrator tells us that students are encouraged to return to their referring school after a minimum mandatory term at EYP.

Overall, the program has more traditional structure and formality than the other alternatives we have seen. There is little opportunity for informal, personal interaction between students and teachers. The program's structure does not provide for students to take "time out" or to relax. At 9:15 the final bell rings and the building is quickly empty.

The Feasibility Study

We were not willing to select programs for study on the basis of their staffs' intentions, their reputations, or our own informal observations. We instituted a feasibility study first, which served several functions. We collected systematic data to determine that the alternative schools did indeed actualize those essential features the theory identified. This enabled us to pretest measures and procedures for later use as well. Also, we and the candidate schools got an opportunity to work together on research to see if we were compatible before the major study began.

We gathered data on the alternative schools by administering questionnaires to their students and by systematically observing classroom interaction. In order to ensure that the alternative schools were different in important respects from the conventional schools that the alternative students had attended, we also collected parallel data at the conventional junior and senior high schools. In order to determine the characteristics of students in the various schools, we searched school, police, and court records, and we questioned the students themselves. As much as possible we employed measures and procedures that had already been proved in related research.

The questionnaires were designed to determine whether from the students' perspective the alternative schools actually provided students with more experiences of success and more warm, personal relations with their teachers. The Classroom Environment Scale (CES) (see Tricket and Moos 1973 and Stern 1970) and Quality of School Life (QSL) (see Epstein and McPartland 1976a, 1976b) measures were selected as the main components of a self-administered, teacher-monitored questionnaire on the grounds of their coverage, validation, and format. Each had been developed and validated on large samples of secondary school students. Administration and response are quite straightforward and simple.

We developed two critical indexes from the questionnaire. One measures teacher-student relations and was adapted from the CES. This measure asks students to indicate whether certain statements are "true" or "false" about a particular class of theirs. Examples of statements are "The teacher takes personal interest in students" and "The teacher is more like a friend than an authority." The other measures students' confidence in their ability to succeed in their school. It includes these statements: "I can learn things at this school," "I can't be successful in this school," and "You just can't win in this school."

These questions, along with many others, were asked of comparable students in the candidate alternative schools and in the conventional schools from which the alternative school students were referred. In order to ensure comparability of the participating students across the two kinds of schools, we determined what curriculum, what track if there were tracks, and what classes the alternative school students had come from, and we enlisted conventional school respondents from these classes. As might be expected, the students tended to come from general rather than college preparatory curricula and from "slow" tracks rather than "fast." We concentrated our efforts on required classes in the conventional schools— mostly English, but some social studies—in order to invoke the broadest cross section of comparable students. Of course, the con-

ventional school participants in this initial phase of our research
were not comparable to the alternative school students in at least
one important respect: most of them had not been singled out for
referral because of their intolerable behavior. Some of them might
have been referred and were awaiting placement and might soon be
referred, but most of the conventional students were accommodating to their schools. We did not at this stage identify especially
troublesome conventional school students. We reasoned that we
would in this way conduct a conservative test of the perceived differences between the alternative and conventional programs. We
assumed that the alternative school students would be more negative about school in general, their teachers, and their chances to
succeed than most students were; and if they were nevertheless
more positive about their alternative programs, then the programs
must certainly be distinctive.

Table 1 presents the number of alternative and conventional

**TABLE 1. Number and Type of Classes Sampled
in Conventional and Alternative Schools**

	Class Type	Classes	Students
System L			
High School 1	English	2	57
	Social Studies	1	25
High School 2	English	9	267
	Social Studies	5	145
Alpha		1	32
High School 3	English	3	68
	Social Studies	2	49
High School 4	English	4	109
	Social Studies	4	112
Beta		1	32
System R			
High School	English	7	162
	Social Studies	8	176
Junior High School 1	English	3	51
	Social Studies	5	125
Junior High School 2	English	4	94
	Social Studies	3	80
ACE		1	15
System W			
High School 1	English	5	110
High School 2	English	5	95
EYP	English	6	101
Total		79	1,905

school students for each of the five programs that responded to our questionnaire. No student refused to participate and only a scattered handful of questionnaires were unusable for some reason.

We examined the data to determine if the students' reports from the two types of schools differed in ways which indicated that the alternative schools were providing more experiences of success and more supportive teacher-student relationships. The findings are displayed in table 2. The "Classroom Affect" variable clearly differentiates the alternative from the conventional schools beyond reasonable probability of chance differences. This means that in each program, the alternative students reported a greater degree of support from their teachers, more personal relationships with them, more dedication to their schoolwork, closer relationships with their classmates, and greater participation in determining how they spend their time in school. But according to the findings concerning "School Success," not all the alternative schools are so clearly different from their feeder conventional schools. Alpha, Beta, and ACE students reported more confidence in their ability to succeed than their conventional counterparts did, but the difference among the ACE students is not statistically reliable; and the difference between the EYP's alternative and conventional students reveals that the conventional students felt reliably more confident of success.

Some background information about the ACE program at the time puts in perspective the unreliable differences in students' confidence in their scholastic ability. The teacher who had provided continuity in the program over the previous three years was on maternity leave when we administered the questionnaire, so a temporary substitute teacher was filling in. Furthermore, the second teaching position in the program was also open. The result was that one substitute teacher taught in the alternative classroom during the period preceding and including our data collection. This situation persisted until after all the data were in, at which time the open position was filled and the teacher on leave returned. Until the permanent teachers were in place, counselors were reluctant to refer many students to ACE, so the number responding to the questionnaire was small and the tenure of several of them had been brief.

So the findings for ACE are probably conservative in relation to its reestablished operation after our data were in. Unfortunately our schedule and resources required that we collect data when the ACE program was in flux.

TABLE 2. Comparison of Alternative and Conventional Schools, Classroom Affect and School Success

	n		Classroom Affect					School Success				
			Alt.		Conv.			Alt.		Conv.		
	Alt.	Conv.	Mean	S.D.[a]	Mean	S.D.[a]	p_{diff}	Mean	S.D.[a]	Mean	Conv.	p_{diff}
Alpha	32	460	1.93	.04	1.61	.21	<.001	1.92	.15	1.88	1.12	<.05
Beta	28	304	1.90	.08	1.54	.21	<.001	1.90	.15	1.82	0.30	<.05
ACE												
High school	14	209	1.67	.15	1.52	.17	<.01	1.92	.15	1.85	0.27	NS[b]
Jr. high school	14	330	1.67	.15	1.54	.20	<.05	1.91	.15	1.79	0.31	NS[b]
EYP	91	186	1.66	.18	1.50	.19	<.001	1.75	.29	1.81	0.29	<.05

[a] S.D. = standard deviation
[b] NS = $p > .05$

Overall, the students' responses to our questionnaire indicated a range in the distinctiveness of the alternative schools. Alpha and Beta were clearly seen by their students to promote both warm, personal relationships between their teachers and themselves and confidence in themselves as students. The EYP did the former, but not the latter. ACE may have been subject to a conservatively biased estimate of its distinctiveness regarding its promotion of students' confidence; the data suggest that ACE fits between Alpha and Beta on the one hand and EYP on the other.

Direct observations of teacher-student interaction provided another perspective on the distinctiveness of the alternative schools. If the programs actually put into practice the theoretically important elements of alternative schooling for disruptive, delinquent youth, then the behavior of the teachers should show it. In the concrete realities of school life, teachers' behavior is the primary differentiating feature for students. So we spent hundreds of hours observing classroom interaction.

The most general decision concerning how to make classroom observations was the choice between an unstructured, impressionistic approach and a structured, objective approach. We wanted to avoid the biases inherent in impressionistic techniques. While impressionistic or ethnographic procedures are most appropriate for some purposes, the comparative nature of our project's task called for a structured, standardized, replicable approach. Obviously, observers would know whether the classes they were observing were in conventional or alternative schools. We wanted to guard as much as possible against their global presumptions about what differences there might be. Having reached that decision, we consulted the literature in search of a standardized classroom observation measure, one appropriate for our sample which would yield information on relevant dimensions.

Out of the plethora of classroom observation measures emerged the Flanders Interaction Analysis Categories (FIAC) (Flanders 1965, 1970). The Flanders scheme has a number of attractive attributes. It is quite straightforward. Only nine substantive categories are used (a tenth records periods of silence or unintelligible interaction), and they are readily learned (see fig. 1). Published training materials and materials for assessing the reliability of observers are available. The FIAC is the most widely used observation scheme in research on education and has been well validated in secondary school settings (see Flanders 1965, 1970; Rosenshine and Furst 1973).

Teacher Talk	Response	1.	*Accepts feeling.* Accepts and clarifies an attitude or the feeling tone of a student in a non-threatening manner. Feelings may be positive or negative. Predicting and recalling feelings are included.
		2.	*Praises or encourages.* Praises or encourages students; says "um hum" or "go on"; makes jokes that release tension, but not at the expense of a student.
		3.	*Accepts or uses ideas of students.* Acknowledges student talk. Clarifies, builds on, or asks questions based on student ideas.
		4.	*Asks questions.* Asks questions about content or procedure, based on teacher ideas, with the intent that a student will answer.
	Initiation	5.	*Lectures.* Offers facts or opinions about content or procedures; expresses his own ideas, gives *his own* explanation, or cites an authority other than a student.
		6.	*Gives directions.* Gives directions, commands, or orders with which a student is expected to comply.
		7.	*Criticizes student or justifies authority.* Makes statements intended to change student behavior from nonacceptable to acceptable patterns; arbitrarily corrects student answers; bawls someone out. Or states why the teacher is doing what he is doing; uses extreme self-reference.
Student Talk	Response	8.	*Student talk-response.* Student talk in response to a teacher contact that structures or limits the situation. Freedom to express own ideas is limited.
	Initiation	9.	*Student talk-initiation.* Student initiates or expresses his own ideas, either spontaneously or in response to the teacher's solicitation. Freedom to develop opinions and a line of thought; going beyond existing structure.
Silence		10.	*Silence or confusion.* Pauses, short periods of silence, and periods of confusion in which communication cannot be understood by the observer.

Fig. 1. Flanders Interaction Analysis Categories. Based on Flanders 1970. No scale is implied by these numbers. Each number is classificatory; it designates a particular kind of communication event. To write these numbers down during observation is to enumerate, not to judge a position on a scale.

The classification of classroom verbal interaction provided by the FIAC seemed appropriate to the task of comparing the alternative and conventional schools. Particularly because categories of teachers "taking the initiative," as well as "giving supportive and confirming responses to students' initiative" were included, these data were expected to complement the perceptions of the students, reported in students' answers to the questionnaire items.

Thirty-six classrooms were observed a total of sixty-seven times. We made no systematic observations in the EYP school or its associated conventional school because the possibility of including them in the study did not occur until it was too late to carry out observations there.

Observers were trained to code one observation in the classroom every three seconds (the usual Flanders procedure) and record this information on standardized coding sheets. The average length of the conventional school class was fifty minutes. The alternative program class meetings lasted two hours. The observation schedules of the observers were evenly distributed over the three alternative programs, five high schools and two junior high schools. An average of 900 to 1,000 three-second observations per session were coded in conventional school classes and approximately 2,200 observations were coded in each two-hour alternative class. Coders were instructed to stop coding when classes took breaks (common in the alternatives) and when films were presented or exams and quizzes given. We tried to arrange observation sessions to avoid times when films or exams were scheduled in order to maximize the probability of observing teacher-student interactions. Time lost to film presentations, etc., was negligible.

The intercoder reliability of observers and their percentage of agreement with an expert standard were computed at the end of the second and third weeks of training and again after all the observations had been completed. Three ten-minute tape recordings of classroom interactions coded by Flanders were used as the expert standard. The rank order correlation (Spearman's rho) was computed for the percentages of responses in each of the ten categories between five observers. At the beginning and end of data collection, no reliability coefficient fell below .87. Percentage of agreement between each individual observer and the Flander's standard was also computed at these times. Percentages ran between 82 and 95 at the start of data collection and 84 and 92 at the end of data collection.

When the observation data collection was completed, initial analyses were performed in which the distributions of category frequencies were examined to be sure they matched the general distributions reported by Flanders. Our distributions were similar to the typical distributions.

Then variables were constructed following Flanders. Categories 1, 2, and 3 were summed to form a Teacher Responds index and categories 5, 6, and 7 were summed into a Teacher Initiates index. We decided to focus our analysis on comparisons between these two indexes and their complementary Student Talk categories (categories 8 and 9). In that way, we were able to concentrate on understanding the response-initiation balance between conventional and alternative school programs. We reasoned that these four measures derived from eight categories represented the types of interactions of greatest relevance and interest. The two remaining categories, "Teacher asks questions" (category 4) and "Silence or confusion" (category 10) were not used beyond preliminary distribution checks.

Figures 2 through 4 show comparisons of each alternative program with its conventional school(s) in terms of frequencies of teacher and student initiation and response. Tests of significance of difference between proportions were computed comparing each alternative and its feeder school(s) on each observation variable. The sum of all the three-second interval observations in each program was used as the base for computing proportions. (In every case, the difference between alternative and conventional classes was significant at the .001 level.)

Compared to the associated conventional school classes, Alpha's and Beta's alternative classes were characterized by a greater proportion of supportive responses by teachers to students' behavior. The higher percentage of response in the alternative programs reflects more praise and encouragement of students' behavior and more frequent occurrence of acknowledgement and acceptance by teachers of the attitudes and feelings expressed by students.

Teachers of the conventional classes on the other hand tended to make more use of their authority and were more critical of students' behavior than the alternative teachers. The higher percentages of teachers initiating interaction in the conventional schools reflects the greater occurrence of teachers lecturing, directing, and exercising authority over the students. This is the other side, as it were, of the alternative teachers' more supportive responses to their students.

Flanders has found that students' learning and perception of their classroom environment can be predicted from observations of the relationship between their talk and the teacher's. More student-

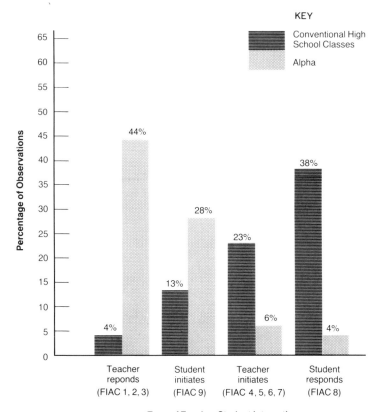

Fig. 2. Comparison of Alpha and its conventional schools, differences in percentage of teacher-student response-initiation balance in Flanders Interaction Analysis Categories (FIAC)

initiated talk is associated with students' perceptions of a supportive classroom environment; fewer student responses in class indicate less teacher-directed behavior. In Alpha and Beta, we found both these relationships. Students' responses were proportionately lower in both alternatives relative to their conventional school, and students' initiating was higher.

In ACE, the proportion of teachers' initiating interaction was less than in the conventional classes, indicating more student-direction (see fig. 3). But the proportion of teachers' responses was also less, indicating less teacher support. We observed that ACE's associated conventional classrooms were characterized by more suppor-

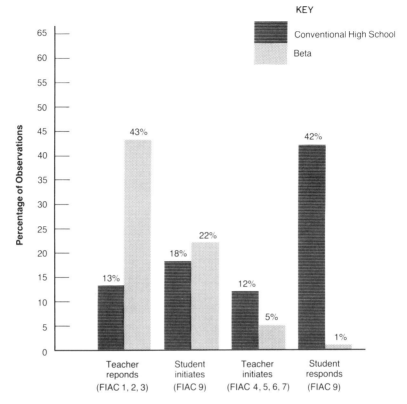

Fig. 3. Comparison of Beta and its conventional schools, differences in percentage of teacher-student response-initiation balance in Flanders Interaction Analysis Categories (FIAC)

tive behavior by teachers than was ACE itself. We attribute this finding to the nature of the alternative program at the time observations were made. Recall that ACE was in a period of uncertainty, staffed by one substitute teacher instead of its usual complement of two permanently assigned teachers. Actually, the substitute spent less time interacting with the students in a manner indicative of attempts to control or direct students' behavior. This is evidenced by the substantially greater proportion of teachers initiating interactions in the conventional school. There appears to have been about half as much control over students' behavior at ACE. We believe that the substitute teacher did not attempt to control ACE students

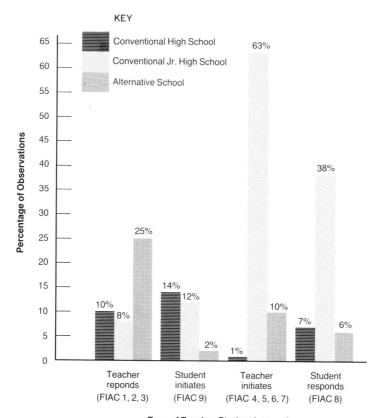

Fig. 4. Comparison of ACE and its conventional schools, differences in percentage of teacher-student response-initiation balance in Flanders Interaction Analysis Categories (FIAC)

so much, but she also did not provide much supportive feedback. This is in part supported by the finding that students initiated more talk in the alternative program than their counterparts did in the conventional high school, a finding which is indicative of students beginning to perceive their environment as more supportive (Flanders 1970).

The relative "newness" of ACE's alternative teacher is also reflected in our finding that over 50 percent of the interaction in the alternative's classes were coded as 10—silence and confusion. ACE's substitute spent the least time of any teacher observed engaged in codable interactions with students. During more than half of the time, the teacher worked with individual students at their seats. Our observers were instructed not to follow the teacher around the room, so these interactions were necessarily but somewhat erroneously coded in category 10. In light of the higher proportion of student initiation, it is plausible that the teacher was responding supportively while engaging in these private interactions. We concluded that the differences in teacher- and student-initiated talk reflected a trend in which teachers' supportive responses would increase with the consolidation of the program's permanent staff (a development which, indeed, occurred).

The data on student initiating interaction at ACE also suggested the trend toward more supportive teacher behavior there. Apparently, the substitute teacher and the students were aware of ACE's philosophy to deemphasize the conventional requirements and constraints of the student and teacher roles, so students felt more free than in the conventional schools to speak out.

One of the assumptions we made when we decided both to question students and observe classroom interactions was that both methods would reflect the same reality. If this is so, then the findings should be related. In order to check into this, we compared questionnaire data on classroom affect with interaction scores. The classroom affect data are more appropriate to this inquiry than are the data on students' confidence in their scholastic ability. This is because the classroom affect data are specific to the same classroom in which the students were observed, while the measure of scholastic confidence pertain to scholastic experiences generally. The relationships between these measures consistently indicate that they do reflect the same reality. In classrooms where students' initiating and teachers' responding were relatively high, students reported more positive relationships with their teachers.

We also compared another variable derived from the students' questionnaire, "classroom maintenance," which tapped students' perceptions of their teachers wanting to keep order in class. (Some items are "If a student breaks a rule in this class, he's sure to get in trouble," "The teacher explains what the rules are," and "We often spend more time discussing outside student activities than class-related material.") We found that the more we observed teachers initiating interaction and students responding, the more students reported that their teachers wanted orderly classrooms. None of the correlations between our observations and students' reports were statistically significant. (N was based on number of classrooms observed, and was thus relatively quite low.) Our opinion that the two methods confirm each other is based on the consistency with which we found agreement among the measures. (See Mann, et al. 1978 for further presentation concerning these relationships.) It is worth noting that the relationships between the two methods of measurement were considerably stronger in the alternative school data than in the conventional school data. It appears that teachers' behaviors were more closely related to students' perceptions in the alternative schools then in the conventional schools. It may be that conventional school teachers' behavior is inconsistent, in two senses: first, these teachers may not interact with all their students in the same general way; second, the teachers may act differently from day to day. Both kinds of inconsistency would make our characterization of teacher-student interaction less valid. The alternative school teachers, on the other hand, were working under conditions which may have made their behavior more consistent: interacting for longer periods of time with a relatively small number of students who were more homogeneous in important respects, and guided by a more or less explicit pedagogical philosophy.

Finally, we discuss our investigation to determine if the alternative schools were really serving significantly more disruptive and delinquent students than the conventional schools.

We searched the police and court records in the appropriate communities for evidence of students' misbehavior. In the case of Alpha and Beta, the assistant principals of the conventional high schools declined to allow us to search police files for names of their students, although our search was done using code numbers so that no one would know which students, if any, had records. The assistant principals did provide us with school disciplinary records instead. It was neither necessary nor desirable, given our resources, to search the records for all of the conventional students. Since the students in comparable conventional classes numbered in the hundreds we selected representative samples of thirty of them at random from each school. We adopted the same strategy for students at EYP, where there were also over thirty students.

Table 3 presents the comparison between the official records of misbehavior of alternative and conventional school students. Court records are not very informative because so few of the students were found there. This is not surprising; very few adolescents acquire court records. Only about half of the youth who are caught for committing delinquencies are referred to court, and of those referred, not all are accepted and acquire court records. And, of course, few of

TABLE 3. Official Records of
Misbehavior Comparing
Alternative and Conventional
School Students, by Program

	Court Records		Police Records	
	%	n	%	n
Alpha				
Alt.	3	1	73[a]	22
Conv.	2	1	28[a]	17
Beta				
Alt.	2	1	60	18
Conv.	7	4	18	11
ACE				
Alt.	50	9	—	—
Conv.	1	1	—	—
EYP				
Alt.	17	5	38	11
Conv.	10	3	16	10

[a] School disciplinary rather than police records

even the heavily delinquent youth are ever caught. So court records are usually scant and not very useful for evaluating programs or assessing the misbehavior of a group of youngsters. Nevertheless, we note for whatever it is worth that a larger proportion of alternative school students appeared in the court records than conventional students did in every program but Beta. The difference in the ACE program is dramatic: 50 percent to 1 percent.

The records of police contacts (or disciplinary contacts in the Alpha comparison) are more numerous and therefore more informative. In each case more alternative than conventional students had contact with the police, by wide, statistically significant margins (beyond the .01 level).

We concluded from these data that all four alternative schools were serving the more disruptive and delinquent students that they claimed to serve and whom we wanted to study.

We also note in these data a caution about research design. The fact that the alternative school students proved to be more troublesome than a representative sample of their former classmates makes the latter a poor comparison group for assessing the effectiveness of alternative schools. Many evaluations of delinquency treatment programs have used just such samples for comparison. But, of course, the students in treatment were selected for treatment because they were different. Even classmates in their tracks in school were not comparable with respect to an important characteristic, their official histories of misbehavior. For this reason, we required that comparable students—students who might have attended the alternative school but could not because classes were filled—be available to our study.

During the course of firming up arrangements to identify conventional school comparison groups for each alternative school, another fact came to our attention that led us finally to drop the EYP from the study. We were able to determine for each alternative school program the proportion of its students who in the previous year had not shown up at all or who had dropped out of school after attending for only a little while. In Alpha, Beta, and ACE, these proportions were around 10 percent. At the EYP, however, fully one-quarter of the referrals never appeared at the school and another 20 percent dropped out before very long. This rate of attrition posed a major problem of research design, for it made the group of students who attended EYP a highly self-selected one. Since we could not identify which of the comparison group would have shown up or dropped out, it would obviously not be a comparable group. Since so few of the other alternative schools' students dropped out, this was not a problem there.

We should point out that the high attrition rate at EYP might not have presented a problem for research design had we been interested in simply evaluating the program. One could argue that one criterion of program effectiveness is its holding power, that attrition rate itself is a criterion. Furthermore, this argument assumes, the evaluation of a program should include all of its clients, even those who dropped out or never even showed up. This argument asserts, with good reason we think, that the referral process and holding power are parts of a program, albeit often ignored.

The counterargument is that referrals who do not appear for the program or who drop out before completing it do not receive sufficient "treatment" to provide a fair test of whether the program works. This argument assumes a narrow view of a program which excludes the referral process and holding power.

Our position is this: If one wants simply to evaluate a program by comparing its results with other program results, these no-shows and dropouts ought to be included for both the substantive and methodological reasons already stated: holding power is an important criterion of program effectiveness; and comparable groups are critical for nonbiased evaluation.

However, this study's aim went beyond program evaluation. As we have stated, we were interested in testing a theory as well. The programs constituted our experimental conditions. Our "subjects"—the students—had to receive adequate exposure to the various conditions in order to provide a test of the theory.

Thus the data from the EYP, unfortunately, presented two reasons for dropping it. Its high attrition rate and its students' pessimism regarding their scholastic success both indicated that the program did not provide the appropriate experimental conditions. We were reluctant to drop EYP from the study because the program was in important ways quite different from the three we retained. It was a large, continuation night school. If that kind of program also really represented the kind of alternative that the theory hypothesizes will be effective, then our test of the theory would have been even more general than it was. It is possible, however, that a large, continuation night school program is inherently unable to be the kind of alternative school the theory prescribes.

Chapter 4

Research Strategies

The design of our study, in technical terms, was a short-term longitudinal experimental/control group design. What that meant specifically in this case was that we intended to observe two sets of young people, those who attended, or were supposed to attend, any of the participating alternative school programs, and those who were referred to the programs but could not attend for reasons independent of their own characteristics. That is, the control students were to be as eligible for an alternative school as the others but for reasons such as the classes being full could not attend. Furthermore, we intended to observe the students before, during, and after the "treatment"; that is, at the beginning of the academic year, at the end, and six months later. (We also intended a follow-up study several years later, but that has not happened.)

Selecting Students for the Study

Inasmuch as Alpha, Beta, and ACE enrolled a small number of students, we decided to include all the alternative school students who were willing to participate. In effect, then, our alternative school population was selected for the study by those procedures which selected students for the programs. So we will describe those procedures first, then the way the comparison groups of conventional school students were built.

Each of the alternative schools was filled using slightly different procedures. The main nominal distinctions were that ACE was filled entirely by students referred to it by conventional school administrators, Beta was filled entirely by students who volunteered for the program, and Alpha was filled half by volunteers and half by referrals.

ACE

ACE served the two junior high schools and the single high school in its school district. Students were formally referred to ACE by their assistant principal, although in the case of high school students, referrals were usually initiated by the counselors. The referrals were typically for disruptive behavior, repeated or serious violation of school rules, or for chronic truancy.

By the time ACE was presented as an option to a student, few other options remained open. The alternative to ACE was usually a two-week disciplinary suspension or being dropped from one or more classes because of more than fifteen absences during a semester. Historically as well as during our observations, only about 5 percent of those offered the option of attending ACE turned it down.

In order to compose a comparison group, we met with the high school counselors and all of the assistant principals involved to work out a procedure for randomly assigning students from among those referred to the ACE program. Arrangements were agreed upon in the spring and were to be implemented in the fall of the 1978–79 school year, the time when the first set of interviews would take place. It was clear from extensive discussions with the ACE administrator, the principals, assistant principals, and counselors that more students could be referred to ACE than ACE could accommodate. The random assignment procedure was based on this excess of need over service capacity. Each of the counselors and assistant principals agreed to refer two or three more students than they might have in the past. Upon receiving a referral, the assistant principal would contact the ACE administrator, who would contact us. We would then use a random number table to determine if the referral should go ahead or be denied. Those denied the referral would remain in their conventional schools. They were to constitute the control group for their peers referred to ACE.

We resolved the ethical problem of denial of service in the following way. The administrators and counselors agreed that there were more students in need of ACE's services than could be served, as just noted. They also agreed that among this group it was really not possible to definitively rank students on the basis of need for ACE's services. Thus, the students who would be denied services under the study's random assignment procedure would have been no more likely to receive services in the absence of the research project. The reason was that, as has been demonstrated in other connections (Dawes 1979), any individual's decisions regarding selection from groups whose members have similar attributes tend to be unreliable: that is, the selections or rankings vary from time to time. This describes the situation of not being able to definitively rank order the most difficult students.

These arrangements were settled in good faith by all concerned, but in the abstract. When the time came in the fall of the year to implement the assignment procedures, they failed to hold up. One junior high school simply made no referrals. The other insisted that most of its referrals bypass the assignment procedure because of the urgency of the cases or because of parental pressure. The high school counselors made many fewer referrals than these same counselors had in years past.

The explanation was the same in all cases. The people involved took seriously their responsibilities for their students. They were reluctant to leave the final disposition of their cases up to chance. Instead, they fashioned other dispositions for their students or insisted on bypassing the assignment procedures. The school principals were aware of our problems. They supported the research project but felt their first responsibility had to be to their staff members and the needs of the students.

These problems did not become clear until well into the fall. Understandings about the assignment procedures were probed and confirmed, but the rate of ACE referrals remained low. The number of (randomly assigned) control students was even lower. We faced the choice at the end of November of sticking to our original control group design at the cost of vitiating our study of ACE, because of a grossly insufficient number of control students, or modifying the design. We chose the latter. We met with the counselors at the high school and, once again, explained our problems. We then asked each of them to nominate up to five of their students for whom they felt the ACE program would be appropriate. We went over the names with each counselor to be sure the students were legitimate candidates for referral. A few names were deleted and the rest were contacted and interviewed in January and February—the beginning of the year's second semester. These students constituted the bulk of the "control" group, now a comparison group, for the ACE program.

Part of the modification of our plans for ACE included terminating the random assignment procedures for the ACE program. At that time, with our comparison group lists in hand, we stopped identifying new students to recruit into the study. We told this to the counselors and assistant principals. At that time, ACE experienced an unusually large number of referrals. This was no doubt due to the end of the restrictions and uncertainties on the referral process which had been imposed by the study's assignment procedures.

The effect of these problems on the kinds of comparability of alternative and conventional school students can be readily summarized. According to the assistant principals and counselors, many of the ACE students were extreme cases whose disruptive behavior could not be tolerated in the school. These cases were too serious for their disposition to be left to chance. On the other hand, most of the comparison students had not been referred to ACE during the first term. Presumably, their high school counselors felt they could be maintained in school or allowed to drop school for part of the semester. One counselor told us that she advised several students with poor grades and attendance to simply stay home for the rest of the term and try again in the second term. Also, several of the nominated comparison group were sent to ACE during the semester change surge in referrals noted above. Nevertheless, the comparison students were, on the whole, less delinquent and disruptive *in the eyes of their counselors*. Actually, as we shall see, they were not.

Another difference between the groups concerned age. Among those ACE students we interviewed, 40 percent were junior high students, compared to only five percent among the comparison group. The delinquency literature (e.g., Gold and Petronio 1980) clearly shows an age-accelerated pattern in delinquent behavior which peaks at early high school age. Thus, as the study went on, the expected level of delinquency should have been increasing among the younger students and decreasing among the older, high school aged students. Both of these factors, age and selection procedures, made for a conservative test of the effects of ACE. For ACE to show an effect in reducing delinquency, it would have to counteract the effects of an overall younger group seen to have been more extreme in their disruptive behavior.

Alpha

Alpha reserved half of its spaces for students who had been referred for poor attendance and disciplinary problems at the two high schools it served. Referred students typically had been dropped from two or more classes because of poor attendance. (Seven unexcused absences in a term constituted grounds for being dropped from a class.) Most of the referred students also presented other discipline problems while in school and usually had poor academic records. Referred students had the option of declining Alpha, although other options were usually limited to being suspended or being dropped from several or all classes for the semester. Less than 5 percent typically refused Alpha, also the case during the course of the study.

Alpha's remaining places were reserved for students who volunteered for the program. The only restriction on volunteers was that they have relatively good records of attendance. Students who had been dropped for poor attendance from more than one class were ineligible to volunteer for Alpha. Most volunteer students were far behind in credits earned, had poor grades, spotty attendance records, and had disciplinary problems at school. They tended to have heard of Alpha from friends or were informally referred to the program by the few counselors positively disposed toward Alpha. Alpha teachers were usually unable to remember which students were referrals and which were volunteers, although they had known initially. The students also seemed unaware of the distinction. We found no differences in any of our initial measures of attitudes and behavior between volunteers and referred students in Alpha.

In each of Alpha's preceding six years, there had been two to five times more volunteers than slots for them. Selection from among the volunteers was by lottery. A public drawing was held to choose each fall's complement of new volunteer Alpha students. The lottery was held during the second or third week of school in the fall. Our plan was to use the applicants not chosen in the drawing as the control group for the Alpha volunteers.

The selection of control students for the referred students was to be similar to that planned for the ACE program. Each of the two high schools had three assistant principals. Each assistant principal was responsible for seeing to the attendance and discipline problems of his or her students and referrals to Alpha had to go through the student's assistant principal. An agreement was made in which each assistant principal would in the fall of 1978–79 school year select the five most likely and appropriate referrals to Alpha. This would make a pool of about twice the open referral slots. Students from this pool to be referred to Alpha by the assistant principals would be selected at random by a member of our research staff. The students not selected would be the controls for those referred.

Neither of these control group selection procedures was successful. Very few students volunteered for Alpha; fewer, in fact, than the number of spaces reserved for volunteers. When it became clear after Alpha's efforts to recruit new students in mid-September that there would not be enough volunteers, these few remaining volunteer spaces were filled by referral students. We thus had no volunteer control group. Fortunately, as we noted, volunteers, referrals, and our comparison groups proved to be comparable on virtually all our measures.

The random assignment procedures for students referred to

Alpha met the same fate as those for ACE, and for the same reasons. The assistant principals felt they had to respond to what they saw as urgent needs of students and pressure from parents to do something. So they insisted on bypassing the random assignment procedures and placing these students in Alpha. By the time we were able to obtain lists from the assistant principals of students from which random assignments could be made, the semester was more than half over and ten of Alpha's twelve open referral slots were filled. We decided to wait until the beginning of the next semester when a few slots in Alpha were expected to open. In the meantime, we worked toward getting a pool of potential referrals from which the few open slots could be filled. From those remaining, we made random selections to fill out the now mixed control/comparison group for Alpha. (Ideally, we would have included all of the nominated students as comparisons, but their number was greater than the number we could afford to interview.)

The result of all of this was that the composition of Alpha and its "control" group was not what we had expected. Alpha had a large proportion of urgent and severe cases who had bypassed the random assignment procedures. There were no such cases in the comparison group. Also, there were fewer volunteers in the program than antici- pated. These two factors combine to make the test of Alpha's effec- tiveness a more conservative one than planned. In that way, it was like ACE. It would have to be effective with students identified as more problematic than those in the comparison group in order to come out superior to the comparison group. Of course, the absence of any volunteers in the comparison group countered this trend, but only to a limited degree. Had the climate in the high schools been more favorable to Alpha, many of those on the comparison group list could well have been encouraged to apply for Alpha.

There are a number of possible explanations for the failure of the agree-upon and planned-for assignment procedures to work out. Alpha did not enjoy good relations with its conventional high schools. Many if not most of the high school counselors and teachers felt it was not a worthwhile program. For students contemplating volunteering for Alpha, there were few sources of positive informa- tion about Alpha among the conventional schools' staff, counselors, and administrators. Students who might be inclined and eligible to volunteer for Alpha tended to be discouraged from doing so. Some assistant principals felt that all of the slots in Alpha should be reserved for referred students, which might explain some of the reluctance to encourage volunteers. Finally, the one remaining original Alpha teacher left for a job outside the school district just after the beginning of the school year. He had always handled relations with the conventional schools as well as liaison with the district administration. It is possible that those in the conventional schools who opposed Alpha felt they could do so more actively after this teacher's departure. Whether or not this actually occurred, the fact remained that Alpha began the year with one new and one experienced staff member. Two weeks into the year, the experienced hand left and was replaced by a teacher/counselor who had bid for the job. He transferred to the Alpha job from his position in one of the high schools which Alpha served. Both of the new staff members were qualified for their new jobs but neither had had experience recruiting students or dealing with an at least somewhat hostile institutional environment.

All of these were factors which may have had an influence on the extremely small number of students who volunteered for Alpha. We cannot weight them as to importance and cannot be sure all of them were important. Nevertheless, we feel we would be remiss in not documenting these circumstances for their value in understanding some of the relationships many alternative schools have with their environments.

Beta

The Beta program was entirely voluntary. As noted in the previous section, students had always signed up for Beta in far greater numbers than could be accommodated. Beta's staff held recruiting meetings in Beta's two conventional high schools during the second week of the school year. Students could apply to go to Beta until a late September deadline following which a lottery was held to select the students to fill the open slots at Beta. Our plan was to use those not chosen in the lottery as controls for those who were chosen.

The two codirectors of Beta had earlier pressed for an expansion of the program's capacity to sixty students divided among three seminars, up from forty students divided between two seminars. The expansion took place for the 1978–79 school year, the beginning of the field work phase of the study. As a consequence, for the first time in Beta's history, there were no "extra" volunteers. All could be accommodated, so all of those who applied for Beta and had parental permission were signed up for the program in late September. At that time, the program was full. We thought that more students would apply to go to Beta during the fall and could be interviewed as controls. This did not happen, and it became clear that we had to modify the design or abandon the site.

Some fourteen students had not followed through on their fall applications to Beta. These were students whose parents did not approve their child's application to Beta. We interviewed these students as members of a comparison group for Beta. We waited for the semester change, hoping that a surplus of volunteers would result from applications for the slots expected to open up at the beginning of the new term. This hope was only partially fulfilled. As earlier, most of the students available as "controls" had not gotten parental permission to attend Beta.

We felt the size of our comparison group, even with these second semester additions, was uncomfortably small. Adding to this concern was the fact that by early into the second term, three students of our earlier comparison group had transferred to Beta. We thus turned with reluctance to nominees. We asked assistant principals to nominate students who met several criteria. They had to be students the assistant principals felt were appropriate for Beta and could benefit from the program. Secondly, they had to have some academic, discipline, and attendance problems, although not especially severe problems. This last condition was added because it seemed to characterize the students already at Beta. We made a random selection of twelve names from the resulting list to fill out the Beta comparison group.

The effects on the research design of the selection of Beta students and their comparison group are difficult to assess. As we will show, the comparison group's aggregate characteristics matched those of the Beta students. Moreover, among the comparison students, the characteristics of the volunteers matched those of the nominees. As noted, ultimately some half-dozen members of the comparison group applied to and were signed up for Beta during the school year. This made for some design problems, but reinforces the use of the comparison group as an appropriate standard against which to assess the effects of Beta.

Recruiting Participants for the Study

As soon as potential respondents were identified to us, we began our attempts to recruit them into the study. The first step was an introductory letter describing the study. We stated in this initial letter that the study was being conducted by the University of Michigan's Institute for Social Research, not by the schools. We also made plain that nobody at the schools or at home would see any individual's answers. Further, the letter stated that we wanted to hear what students had to say and that we were interested in all sides of the story about school, the good and the bad. We emphasized that the study would give our respondents a chance to be heard and to make a difference in how schools were run. The letter mentioned that while we couldn't pay cash money for their help, we would be able to give respondents scrip redeemable at McDonald's, Inc., restaurants in exchange for participation in the interview. The letter closed with an indication that a phone call from the study would be forthcoming. The purpose of the call was, as stated, to answer any questions and to try to arrange for an interview appointment.

All the calls for each wave of interviews were made by only one person per wave—that wave's scheduler. This was intended to help rapport in cases where multiple calls had to be made to the same household as well as to preserve information and assure consistent procedures. The study was also explained to parents during these phone calls. The scheduler was persistent in her attempts to contact potential respondents or to schedule an interview appointment for those respondents who in earlier calls had indicated they might be able to schedule an appointment at a later date.

When the scheduler encountered clear signs of resistance or hostility, a second letter was composed and sent. Its object was to assuage fears or address the concerns which had been voiced (usually by the parents). Depending on the case, a follow-up telephone call might also have been made. These procedures were uniformly unsuccessful in persuading parents or potential respondents to relent.

The second wave of interviews began in May of 1979 and was largely completed by mid-July. The second interview was introduced by a letter which stressed many of the same points made in the first letter. The letter also noted that even though some respondents might have stopped going to school, we still sought their views. A newspaper story about the study was reproduced and enclosed. The story described the study's potential contribution to the education policy-making process and emphasized the role of students' views in shaping the study's findings. This letter closed as did the first, mentioning the same incentive and telling the respondent to expect a call from the study to make arrangements for the interview.

Our recruiting efforts for the third wave were directed at all of the potential respondents originally identified at the study's outset.

Its introductory letter stressed the importance of follow-up information for applying the study's findings. Also mentioned were the reports of the study's results made to state, local, and national groups.
For reasons to be described, we had increased the incentive from
fast-food chain scrip to five dollars cash. The cash incentive was
mentioned in the letter as was the forthcoming call to schedule the
interview. Additional letters were sent and phone calls made to
reluctant respondents or their parents, again with little success. We
sent members of our field staff out to the last known addresses of
respondents we had been consistently unable to contact by phone. In
a few cases, this resulted in interviews or in information as to the
whereabouts of the potential respondent which ultimately resulted
in interviews. Interviews were conducted by telephone with three
respondents who had moved out of state.

Response Rates

The base number for figuring response rates is 240, the total
number of alternative and conventional school students initially
identified to us by the schools at the outset of the study. Of those,
100 (42 percent) were originally alternative school students. The
remaining 140 (58 percent) were in conventional schools when the
study began.

The cross-sectional and compound response rates for the three
waves of the study are given in table 4. The dip in response rates at
wave 2 and the alternative students' higher response rates are the
notable features in the table. Competition from warm, sunny spring
weather may have also accounted for some of the decrement in response at wave 2. The unavoidably brief interval for many respondents between the first and second interviews might also have
affected the wave 2 response rate. Adding five dollar "incentive pay"
at the third wave may have contributed to the better rate at that
time.

We were able to make personal appeals for participation in the
study to most of the alternative students during our visits to their
programs. We answered questions and discussed the study (in ap-
propriately general terms) with the alternative students. The comparison students were not similarly accessible to us, dispersed as
they were through many classes in many schools. The alternative
students were in general probably more committed to the study
since they were in general more committed to their schools. The
alternative teachers were interested in seeing their programs evaluated by neutral observers and so encouraged their students to par-

TABLE 4. Cross-sectional and Compound Response
Rates, Overall and for Alternative and Conventional
Students

	Overall	Alternative	Conventional
Base	240	100	140
Wave 1			
Interviewed	180	83	97
% response	75%	83%	69%
Wave 2			
Interviewed	140	65	75
% response	58%	65%	54%
Wave 3			
Interviewed	161	72	89
% response	67%	72%	64%
Compound rates			
W1 × W2 × W3	29%	39%	24%
W1 × W2	44%	54%	37%
W2 × W3	39%	47%	35%
W1 × W3	50%	60%	44%

ticipate. All of these factors contributed to the differences in response rates.

Table 5 presents the cross-sectional response rates for each alternative program and its comparison group.

The only notable feature in this table is ACE's lower response

TABLE 5. Cross-sectional Response Rates,
Alternative Programs and Comparison Groups

	ACE	Comp.[a]	Alpha	Comp.	Beta	Comp.
Base	21	53	28	41	51	46
Wave 1						
Interviewed	14	37	25	30	44	30
% response	67%	70%	89%	73%	86%	65%
Wave 2						
Interviewed	11	26	21	23	32	25
% response	52%	49%	75%	56%	63%	54%
Wave 3						
Interviewed	11	34	22	25	39	30
% response	52%	64%	79%	61%	76%	65%

[a] Of the 53 ACE comparison students, 5 were from junior high school. Of these, 2 were interviewed in waves 1 and 2. They were in high school at wave 3.

rates compared to its comparison group in waves 1 and 3. We can shed little light on this reversal. ACE's response rate was stable between waves 2 and 3. The small number of cases from which to draw, a function of the reluctant referral agents, makes further interpretation difficult.

Overall, the response rates were quite good. The wide variation in date of first interview and the consequently variable interval between waves 1 and 2 detract from the usefulness of the wave 2 data. The wave 1 to wave 3 interval was proportionally much less variable. Fortunately, these two time points yielded the best response rates cross-sectionally as well as jointly.

Interviewing and Other Data Collection

Three personal interviews with the students provided most of the study's data. The timing of the interviewing periods and the interviewing procedures will be described in this section. Several noninterview sources of data were also tapped, and these will be noted. Our procedures for obtaining consent and for protecting the confidentiality of the study's participants will also be noted.

Interview Timing

The first interview was to be in the fall of 1978 as that year's new alternative students were entering the programs. This interview asked about the respondents' present (for comparison students) or previous (for alternative students) *conventional* school, as well as about current attitudes and behavior at home and in the community. It provided baseline measures against which to assess change in attitudes, plans, and behavior.

We expected the first wave of interviews to begin in late September, 1978, and to be completed by the end of November, 1978. As described earlier, this did not work out. It was not until February, 1979, that we received from the schools the full final set of names of comparison students for Alpha and ACE. It was not until March, 1979, that we received the final set of names to use as Beta's comparisons.

The progress of interviewing in waves 2 and 3 was under the control of the study instead of dependent on information from the schools. These two waves of interviewing went smoothly and were completed in close to the anticipated eight-week period, with 95 percent done within the specified times.

Administering the Interviews

Our interviewing procedures were designed to make the respondents comfortable and relaxed. To this end, we recruited interviewers who were young in appearance and who could relate easily to adolescents. Most of our interviewers were graduate or undergraduate students or others in their early to mid-twenties. They typically had had recent experience working with adolescents. Interviewers and respondents were matched by sex. The interviews themselves were held in "neutral" sites in the community, either a YWCA or library conference room or an unused elementary school classroom. This was done to insure privacy, reinforce our promise of confidentiality, and minimize interruptions or distractions which might result from conducting the interviews in respondents' homes. Some respondents or their parents, about a third in all, preferred to have the interviews held in their homes. Interviewers rarely reported problems or distractions in these circumstances. Interviews usually took place after school, though respondents' schedules often required morning, evening, and weekend interviews.

The study's field schedule meant that there was turnover among the interviewers between waves—more between the second and third. Continuity in training and procedures was enhanced by two interviewers who worked in all three waves. There was no effort to match or avoid matching interviewers and respondents across waves.

The interviews lasted an average of just over 84 and 82 minutes in waves 1 and 3, and 73 minutes in wave 2. The range of interview length was from 45 to 170 minutes.

Noninterview Data

Supplementary information was obtained from the schools, local police agencies, and the juvenile court in whose jurisdiction the research was conducted. The most extensive noninterview data were provided by the schools.

Dates of enrollment in the alternative schools were obtained for all of the respondents, enabling us to check our information on who attended alternatives and for how long. The schools also provided us with students' official grades for semesters roughly coinciding with waves 1 and 3. Assistant principals tallied their disciplinary contacts with study respondents by type of contact. Finally, we obtained behavior and decorum ratings from the conventional school teachers of all the students in the study after most of the alternative school students had returned to their conventional schools (wave 3).

Local police agencies provided us with an account of the type and date of occurrence of offenses committed by our respondents which resulted in the respondents' names being entered in the agencies' record systems. We obtained similar information plus disposition information from the juvenile court with jurisdiction over the study's geographic area.

Note that in all of the procedures, we were sensitive to potential harm to our respondents. We were, for example, careful to describe our study to the police as an evaluation of different kinds of school programs and that measures of the programs' effectiveness included the level of the students' troublesome behavior. In seeking discipline information from assistant principals and ratings from teachers, the names of alternative and conventional students were freely mixed on the lists. We expressed interest in the data as outcome information pertinent to the schools' as well as our own interests in assessing program effectiveness.

Consent and Confidentiality

Written parental consent was not required for respondents to participate in the study. Nevertheless, in the cases when parents did not consent to their child's participation, the child did not participate.

In order to obtain information from the schools' archives and personnel, we had to have explicit written parental consent. For individuals for whom we did not have written consent, information from the schools was given anonymously. That is, the finest level of identification allowed was by group (for example, girls who had attended alternative schools).

We anticipated that consent would be difficult to obtain considering the population and the necessity of relying on return mail. (We mailed out a request for cooperation, a consent form, and stamped return envelope.) We ultimately received consent to examine records from the parents or guardians of 56 percent of our respondents. This was achieved by separate mailings in the spring and fall of 1979 along with follow-up letters and telephone calls following the fall mailings.

In addition to standard precautions to protect respondent confidentiality, we obtained a Certificate of Confidentiality from the (then) U.S. Department of Health, Education and Welfare. This certificate protected the study staff and materials from any subpoeona or administrative action which might result in identifying any of our respondents. We were thus able to tell our respondents that their answers were protected by law.

Characteristics of Respondents

Comparisons of alternative and conventional school participants are important for assessing how closely we were able to approximate our intended research design. That is, they indicate how similar the comparison and alternative groups were at the outset of the study, at least according to our measures. Ideally, with perfect random assignment of respondents to the two types of schools, the comparison and alternative groups would be identical at the beginning of the study. Any differences in outcomes could then be attributed to the differences in school experiences over the course of the study. Especially since we were unable to achieve random assignment, we needed to make sure that the alternative and conventional school participants were similar.

The following descriptions are based on respondents to the wave 1 interview. We will place the students in context before comparing the two groups.

Demographic Characteristics

Our respondents averaged sixteen years of age at wave 1. The age range was from thirteen to eighteen. There were slightly more girls than boys in the study, ninety-three to eighty-seven. The average grade level was tenth grade. The average point average reported by our respondents for the semester preceding the wave one interview was D+. Eighty-three percent reported having been expelled or suspended from school or sent to the office during the same period.

The two school districts participating in the study were virtually all white and all of our respondents identified themselves as white. We relied on respondents' reports of their fathers' education as a rough index of socioeconomic status. (The respondents were unable to provide detailed information on the nature of their parents' work.) The communities themselves were fairly homogeneous socioeconomically. The school attendance areas tended to be even more homogeneous. Almost two thirds (64 percent) of our respondents reported that their fathers had a high school education or less. The communities in the study were middle-income blue to white collar. Sixty-one percent of our respondents reported living with both natural parents.

We can assess some aspects of the adjustment and behavior of our respondents against norms from representative national samples. The 1972 National Survey of Youth (NSY) (Gold and Reimer 1975) and 1967 data from the Youth in Transition study (YIT) (Bachman, Kahn, Mednick, Davidson, and Johnston 1967) provided data from representative national samples on measures which were identical or almost identical to measures we used. These measures included assessments of self-esteem, anxiety, attitude toward school, commitment to the· student role, and self-reported delinquent behavior.

Self-Esteem and Adjustment

YIT was a longitudinal study of boys only, and began with a representative national sample of tenth graders. This of course limits our normative comparisons. The mean self-esteem scores for the YIT tenth-grade boys and for our sample of boys were exactly the same. Comparisons of our eleventh- and twelfth-grade male respondents with YIT respondents in their eleventh- and twelfth-grade years yielded insignificant differences: our boys were "normal" in their initial self-esteem scores on this measure.

Another measure of self-esteem was also used in NSY, a cross-sectional study whose sample was representative of Americans between the ages of eleven and eighteen years. We compared boys and girls separately. Once again, we found no significant difference between our respondents and the normative group. Our respondents were "normal" according to this measure of self-esteem as well.

We used the Social Self-Esteem test (See Mann 1980; Wylie 1974) as our measure of unconscious self-esteem, replicating its use in NSY. We compared the scores for boys and girls in our study with appropriate scores in the NSY data set. On both comparisons, our respondents' scores were significantly higher in unconscious self-esteem than the normative groups.

Our interview also included a replicate measure of anxiety used in NSY. Splitting both NSY and our respondents by sex, we compared average anxiety scores in the two data sets. The findings for boys showed no reliable differences between our boys and the NSY boys. On average, however, our girls reported more symptoms of anxiety.

Generally, our respondents can be considered normal in almost all respects that we measured. It should be noted however that, contrary to some of the theory we were testing, their unconscious self-esteem was high.

School-Related Attitudes

The NSY and YIT data sets provide normative comparison measures of two school-related attitudes. We asked our respondents to answer in terms of their previous conventional school experience if they were in an alternative program at wave 1. We made separate comparisons for tenth and eleventh graders. There were no differences between our boys and the YIT normative sample of tenth-grade boys in how close they felt they were to doing their best work. Our eleventh graders, however, felt they were not working as close to their ability as did the YIT respondents. Our tenth- and eleventh-grade respondents felt they did not work as hard in school as others. Similarly, our tenth- and eleventh-grade respondents were less satisfied with their performance in school than were the YIT respondents. (Our boys and girls were insignificantly different on these measures.)

The NSY interview included a measure of global attitude toward school which we replicated in our interview. There were no reliable sex differences in either data set. Our respondents were markedly more negative toward school.

Summing up these data, the overwhelming impression is that our respondents were extremely and consistently negative in their attitudes toward school, commitment to the role of student, and their relationships with teachers. They fit the description of the disaffected student. The next data to be reported show them to fit the description of delinquent students as well.

Delinquent Behavior

How deliquent were the respondents in our study? Were the problems they represented troublesome only in relation to otherwise tranquil schools and communities, or could they be considered more generally and genuinely difficult adolescents? Our interview replicated ten delinquency items used in the YIT study. We compared our boys' data with those of YIT and found more of our respondents had: run away from home (30 percent versus 15 percent); used alcohol illegally (92 percent versus 50 percent); been involved in fighting (62 percent versus 35 percent); stolen a car, even if later returned (36 percent versus 12 percent); been in trouble with the police (69 percent versus 34 percent); purposely damaged school property (48 percent versus 28 percent); violated school smoking rules (73 percent versus 21 percent); and been truant (98 percent versus 43 percent). Our respondents also reported more instances of doing serious injury to another and extorting property with threats of injury, but only slightly more frequently than in the YIT data. It should also be noted that except for car theft and fighting, our *girls* reported more delinquency than did the YIT's *boys!*

These data indicate that our respondents were consistently and substantially more involved in delinquent behavior than a representative national sample. As such, they can be considered adolescents whose behavior would be seen as generally troublesome and cause for some kind of preventive or ameliorative action.

Comparisons between Alternative and Conventional School Students

The final set of comparisons examines the similarity of the two groups of students in the study. The kinds of questions these analyses were designed to answer were these: Were the comparison students initially comparable to the alternative students so that comparisons of outcomes could be made? How about these comparisons for specific alternative schools? And, were students who were referred to the alternative schools similar to those who volunteered?

The reader should bear in mind that all of the analyses to be reported in this section employ wave 1 data, collected when the alternative school students had only recently entered the programs. That is, they indicate characteristics of respondents at the *outset* of the study. Because we sought baseline data, we told alternative school students to answer for the *conventional* school they recently attended. This allowed us to make sensible baseline comparisons of attitudes toward and experiences in school at wave 1 for respondents who were attending either alternative or conventional schools.

We tested for demographic differences among the various groups, looking particularly at age and sex. We also looked for differences in experiences at school, including grade point average and behavior, and attitudes toward school. Tests of comparability in self-esteem, adjustment, and delinquency completed the variables used in this group comparison analysis.

The demographic comparisons are shown in table 6. The alternative students were, on average, slightly younger than the comparison students. This difference is attributable almost entirely to

TABLE 6. Demographic Characteristics
of Alternative and Comparison Respondents
at Wave 1

Characteristics	Alternative Respondents	Comparison Respondents
Age		
Mean	15.9	16.1
S.D.[c]	1.11	0.86
n	84	96
$p < .01$		
Sex		
% boys	43	53
n	84	99
$p = $ NS		
Discipline History[a]		
% disciplined	82	83
n	77	96
$p = $ NS		
Grade Point Average[b]		
Mean	2.85 (D+)	2.89 (D+)
S.D.[c]	9.43	8.47
n	81	96
$p = $ NS		

[a] Sent to office, suspended, expelled
[b] 1 = F, ... 5 = A
[c] S.D. = standard deviation

the younger students in ACE, those who came from the district's two junior high schools. Nevertheless, the alternative and conventional students were still quite similar. The sex ratio in the two groups was not statistically different. There was a slightly smaller proportion of boys among the alternative students, but overall both groups had about equal proportions of boys and girls.

As to two important indicators of their recent experiences in school, the groups did not differ. Most respondents in each group had been subject to disciplinary action at school. The grade point average of the two groups of respondents was not different, either. Their averages were poor, at about the D+ level.

Initial similarity in the personal adjustment and self-esteem of the two groups was especially important because of the study's guiding theoretical framework. We compared the alternative and conventional school students in terms of their conscious and unconscious self-esteem, anxiety, depression, attitudes toward school, and delinquent behavior. None of the measures of affective states showed a statistically significant difference between the mean scores of the alternative respondents compared with the conventional respondents at the beginning of the study. Their comparability in regard to attitudes toward school was mixed. There were no reliable differences between alternative and conventional students on the global measures of attitude toward school and commitment to the student role. As noted earlier, we found both sets of our respondents to be more negative toward school than normative samples. On the measures of their chances for scholastic success, feelings of personal stigma, and perceptions of relationships with their teachers, the alternative students were significantly more negative than the comparison students at the initial interview. Recall that these questions were answered in reference to the alternative students' previous conventional schools.

We suspect that the differences in the school-related measures are an artifact. That is, virtually all of the alternative students were interviewed after their arrival at the alternative school. In many cases the interviews took place several weeks or more after a student began at the alternative schools. (The delays were due to problems we experienced in initial identification, recruiting, or scheduling of respondents.) So, even though we asked alternative school respondents to respond to these items in terms of their previous conventional school, they could not ignore that they had already in fact been removed or had removed themselves from their old schools, and they had some idea of what their new schools were like. Consider the conventional school histories of these students now in alternative schools and the organization, philosophy, and operation of the alternatives. By comparison, the conventional schools must have sunk even lower in their estimation. On the other hand, the respondents who remained in their conventional schools had no other kind of school to use as a standard of comparison. The possibility of a contextual effect is reinforced by the nature of the questions which show an alternative-comparison difference, for example; "I almost never expect to do well in the classes the school makes me take"; "The teachers and principals don't want me in their school"; and, "Teachers go out of their way to help students." These items tend to be specific, referring to personalities or practices in school. As such, they could easily be affected by a contrasting context. By comparison, the attitudes toward school and the student role measures are more durable and general and less tied to the specifics of any given school, for example, "How satisfied are you with the way you're actually doing in school?" and "How much do you like school in general?" These items are less likely to be affected by relatively brief exposure to a new educational context—brief in comparison with eight to eleven years of previous schooling.

But, what if these initially more negative attitudes of the alternative school respondents were "real"? To the extent (if any) that they reflect actual preexisting differences between the groups, perhaps as a consequence of the selection procedures, such a difference might make for a more stringent, conservative test of the effectiveness of the alternative programs. Although complete comparability would have been ideal, differences which might tilt the findings in a more conservative direction are preferable to those that might compete with or exaggerate explanations of program effectiveness. On the other hand, these initial differences alerted us to the possibility of a statistical "regression effect" whereby the more extreme negativity of the alternative school students would shift toward the average regardless of the program. We took this possibility into account when we analyzed the data on change.

The final comparisons in this series contrasted the delinquent behavior of the two groups. As shown in table 7, the alternative and

TABLE 7. Mean Number of School-Related and General Delinquent Acts of Alternative and Comparison Respondents at Wave 1

Delinquent Behavior[a]	Alternative Respondents	Comparison Respondents
School-Related		
Mean	4.49	3.95
S.D.[b]	2.30	1.98
n	83	92
t value (df = 173) = 1.50, p = NS		
General	1.79	1.58
Mean	0.92	0.79
S.D.[b]	83	92
n		
t value (df = 173) = 1.51, p = NS		

[a] Computed as total occurrences over all acts divided by number of potential acts presented to respondent. Mean is of act occurrences.

[b] S.D. = standard deviation

comparison students were not reliably different in their involvement in delinquent behavior up to the time of the first interview. The difference between the size of the averages for school and nonschool delinquencies reflects two things. First, relatively minor or nonserious behaviors, such as smoking or talking in class, constitute disruptive behaviors in most schools. In that sense, it is easier to get in trouble in school compared with, say, fighting with somebody, stealing from a store, or taking a car. Second, a youngster would have to be quite busy to run up a high number of occurrences of *each* of the 18 general delinquent behaviors, but could still be heavily delinquent by engaging in a relatively small average number of acts.

Comparability within Programs

The next analyses involved the same demographic, affective, and school-related variables as those used to make aggregate comparisons between alternative and conventional schools. Respondents were grouped according to their school program at wave 1 and compared.

Considering the demographic variables first—age, sex, discipline, and grade point average—several findings stand out (table 8). ACE students were younger on average than their conventional counterparts, and Beta students were older. There were proportionately fewer boys at ACE than remained in the conventional school. We found no significant differences in school discipline history.

TABLE 8. Comparisons of Alternative and Conventional/Comparison Group Students on Age, Grade Point Average, Sex, and Discipline Records (Wave 1), by Program

	n^a	Average Age	Sig. Diff.	Average GPA (1.0–5.0)	Sig. Diff.	Boys (%)	Sig. Diff.	Discipline Records (%)	Sig. Diff.
ACE									
Alt.	14	14.6	<.01	2.1	—	36%	<.05	79%	—
Conv.	38	16.0		2.4		68		77	
Alpha									
Alt.	26	16.3	—	3.1	—	23	—	78	—
Conv.	28	16.4		3.2		37		75	
Beta									
Alt.	44	16.1	<.05	3.0	—	57	—	88	—
Conv.	30	15.9		3.2		48		90	

[a] n varies slightly from one measure to another on account of missing data

Within-program differences on the affective measures were scattered and generally inconsistent across the programs. On these measures, the programs were essentially similar.

The only salient feature of the comparisons concerning school-related attitudes involves ACE. ACE students were on the average more negative about their chances for success than their comparison group. The overall greater negativity of the alternative school students that we reported earlier is mainly attributable to their difference in ACE.

Referrals versus Volunteers

We also checked to be sure that respondents who volunteered for the alternative programs, respondents who were referred to alternatives, and comparison respondents were not systematically different. We used procedures analogous to those reported above to test for possible volunteer-referral effects.

We found few differences between the volunteer and referred alternative school students. Those we did find were largely attributable to differences already reported. For example, all ACErs were referred to ACE. They represented about one-half of the study's referred students. Thus, the relative youth of the ACErs and grading policy differences between ACE's district and the Alpha-Beta district resulted in age and grade point average differences between volunteers and referrals. In addition, there was a slightly higher proportion of girls among the referrals compared to the volunteers.

Altogether, there is little to suggest noncompatibility between the volunteer and referral groups. Our later analysis therefore ignored the distinction.

To summarize, the respondents were white boys and girls residing in middle-income suburbs of Detroit. Most of them were high school students who had poor grades, poor attendance records, and otherwise behaved so badly at school that they were about to be excluded. Their behavior outside of school placed them on the average among the 20 percent most delinquent adolescents in the country. Except for their delinquency, they did not seem as a group especially anxious or disturbed. In fact many seemed to enjoy an unusually high level of unconscious self-esteem. A somewhat smaller proportion of them may have been living with both natural parents than were youth in the country as a whole.

The alternative school students and the comparison group of

conventional students were similar in terms of sex ratios, grade point averages, and school disciplinary records. The students at ACE were as a group younger than their conventional school counterparts. Alternative and conventional school students displayed similar psychological adjustment and levels of delinquent behavior. They also had about the same negative attitudes toward school. But the alternative students, when we interviewed them initially, described themselves as having been much poorer conventional school students scholastically and in terms of relationships with their teachers than the conventional students did.

Measures

Delinquency

As much as possible, we borrowed and if necessary adapted already proved measures of the variables we were interested in. The key outcomes, delinquent and disruptive behavior, were measured in several ways. The one we relied upon most were the self-reports of the students. In the course of each of our three interviews with them, we gave them a check list of disruptive and delinquent behavior and asked them to tell in this way what they had done in recent months. This self-report measure was adapted from previous studies where it proved to be reliable and valid (see, for example, Bachman, O'Malley, and Johnston 1978; Gold and Reimer 1975). In addition, at the end of the study we asked teachers in the conventional schools to rate the behavior of their students (among whom were those who had attended alternative schools in the previous year), using a set of items adopted from *Who Becomes Delinquent?* by D. J. West and D. P. Farrington (1973). And we also had the local juvenile court records searched for the names of our participating students.

Self-Esteem and Adjustment

Our measures of self-esteem and personal adjustment had also been already developed in previous research. To measure self-esteem at conscious levels of awareness, we employed the checklist that Jerald Bachman and his associates (Bachman, O'Malley, and Johnston 1978) adapted from the work of Morris Rosenberg (1965). The students were asked to indicate whether they felt that they were "useful person[s] to have around," "take a positive attitude" toward themselves, and so on. To measure self-esteem at unconscious levels, we used a projective test, the Self–Social Construct Test developed by Robert Ziller and his associates (1969; also see

Mann 1981). This test had the students place "yourself" in well-defined spatial relations to "someone who is happy," ". . . a failure," and several other reference points. Our measure of anxiety among adolescents asked the students how frequently they experienced such physical discomfort as headaches and stomachaches. We also used items from the State-Trait Anxiety Inventory (Spielberger 1970). To measure depression, we adapted the Center for Epidemiological Studies Depression Scale (Radloff 1977), asking for example how often students "enjoy life" or "can't shake off the blues."

Attitudes toward School

The particular theoretical orientation of our study required that we construct measures of students' perceptions of and attitudes toward school and the role of student. With regard to perceived flexibility and fairness of the school environment, we were specifically interested in whether the alternative schools struck the students as places where they were less likely to be in trouble and hassled about the rules than in the conventional schools. In our interviews and visits to the schools, our respondents told us that the number, fairness, appropriateness, and equitable enforcement of the rules were important to them. Many reported feeling picked on or set up by the rules in the conventional schools; or that the rules themselves were fair enough but they were administered in a mean, arbitrary, or inflexible manner. Indeed, an assistant principal in one of the conventional high schools told us that he would like to be more flexible in applying or selectively ignoring the rules and sanctions in the school's code of student conduct. He went on to say that he couldn't, however, because the school's faculty would not stand for it. Other high school assistant principals indicated that they did not feel so constrained, but neither were they completely free to handle each case as they saw fit. As noted earlier, the alternative school staffers also felt rules were important symbols of how the school regarded the student. They kept formal rules to a minimum and adopted a flexible approach to infractions or problematic behavior.

We measured students' perceptions of fairness and flexibility in the schools with a series of five questions. They assessed students' satisfaction with the relative involvement of administrators, teachers, and students in making the rules, and their view of the fairness, number, appropriateness, and evenhandedness of enforcement of the rules.

Self as Student

Other measures were constructed to assess different facets of the student role. One measure combined students' feelings of being stigmatized in school with perceived chances for scholastic success in school. The measures of success and stigma were strongly associated with each other, both statistically and conceptually. We combined them into a single measure reflecting the students' sense of their academic prospects.

A related measure was constructed by combining the measure of commitment to the academic role of student and the students' report of their most recent grade point average. These two measures were also strongly associated with each other statistically and conceptually. This index measures seriousness of engagement as a student: how much effort is being put out, the level of performance, and satisfaction with the role.

The final school-related measure tapped the nonacademic side of the school experience. As might be expected, aspects of the academic and nonacademic roles were related to each other. Nevertheless, we felt there was conceptual and statistical merit in separate treatment for the measures of the nonacademic role. There were two components to the measure of students' feelings about nonacademic aspects of school: general attitude toward or liking for school; and the perceived supportiveness of teacher. The attitude measure combined the items about attitude toward school, interest and feelings at the end of the school day, and the attractiveness of activities at school. Questions about teachers included asking how many teachers the respondent liked, the importance respondents ascribed to teachers' views of them, and the helpfulness of teachers. The resulting measure broadly reflected students' attitudes about school. Its content ranged from how a day in school left them feeling about themselves to how frequently they engaged in the school's activities. It emphasized the personal side of relationships with teachers and also included more general attitudes toward school. We consider it to be a global consequence of the social and academic experiences in school on the students' attraction to the institution.

Chapter 5

Findings

A summary of what we found should focus on three questions. First, did the alternative schools work? Did they reduce the disruptive and delinquent behavior of their students relative to the students in the comparison groups who remained in the conventional school program? This question has to do with what has recently come to be called a summative program evaluation. In brief here, yes, the alternative schools worked in the sense that their students showed a marked, statistically reliable decline in their disruptive behavior at school by the time most of them returned to their conventional schools.

Second, to what social psychological processes is the effectiveness of the programs attributable? What ingredients of the programs and what of students' psychological responses to them were responsible for producing change? This question involves testing the theory of alternative schools that led us to observe the particular programs in this study and to measure the variables that we did. Again briefly, the findings provide strong support for most but not all of the theory. It turns out that the kinds of attitudes students had about themselves and toward their school that we believed would be important for change in their behavior were indeed associated with change; but in one respect, regarding unconscious elements of self-esteem, the data do not support the theory.

Third, under what special conditions, if any, did the programs prove effective and the theory prove valid? Here we are concerned with differences among the students when they entered the alternative programs that may have enhanced or diminished the effect of the programs. We found that students who at their first interview evidenced unusually strong signs of anxiety and depression were not enduringly affected by the alternative schools. The programs' enduring effectiveness was limited to those students who, according to our theory, were successfully using disruption and delinquency to defend against psychic pain. The alternative schools did not succeed with those students whose delinquency upon entrance did not appear to help them avoid manifest anxiety and depression. Further, the programs were particularly effective with those less anxious and depressed students who were most delinquent and disruptive at the outset.

In the rest of this chapter, we will present the data and describe in some detail how the alternative students responded to their school experiences differently from the way conventional school students did; how these responses were linked to changes in their behavior; and how the psychological adjustment of the students made a difference in the effects of the alternative program.

General Trends in Behavior over Time

First of all, some findings about the trends in disruptive and delinquent behavior among all the youths in the study. There was a general decline in problematic behavior over the twelve to fourteen months that we observed the youngsters (see figs. 5 and 6). This general decline is not surprising for two reasons. First, other studies have shown that some "maturational reform" is to be expected in a group of highly disruptive youngsters, simply with the passage of

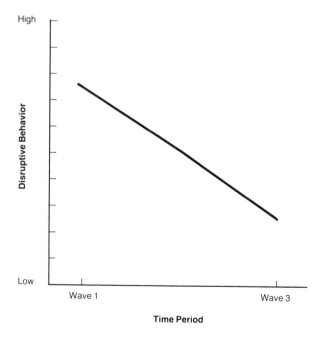

Fig. 5. Change in disruptive behavior at school, all students ($n = 89$)

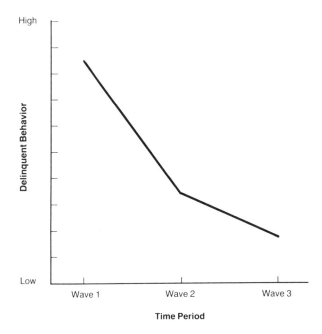

Fig. 6. Changes in delinquent behavior in the community, all students (*n* = 112)

time. Second, any group of youth observed first at such a high level of disruptive behavior that they had to be removed from their schools will on the average settle down somewhat in the normal course of events. The mission of a special program is to maximize and accelerate this benign trend so that problematic students will come even more closely to resemble well-behaved citizens, and sooner. It should be pointed out here that this typical decline is one of the major reasons for including a comparison or control group in a program evaluation. For if some decline is to be expected in any case, then any program might seem effective if viewed in isolation.

Comparison of the Behavior of Alternative and Conventional School Students

The comparative analyses of our data began with a further check on whether the selected alternative schools still differed in hypothetically crucial ways from their counterpart conventional schools. These analyses were similar to the ones we had done earlier in selecting the programs. At this point, however, we used the more elaborate set of measures that are possible in personal interviews but not in self-administered questionnaires; and we compared alternative school students with the particular comparison groups we had identified instead of with all students in certain conventional school classes.

Having determined that the two kinds of school were distinctive, we then analyzed the outcome data to see if the distinctive alternative school experience had a made a difference in the disruptive and delinquent behaviors of the students a year and a half later in comparison to the conventional school groups. We found that there were some marked differences.

Then we traced the social psychological links between attending an alternative school and the behavioral outcomes, guided by our theory. We asked the data whether the intermediate causal linkages that we believed would occur did in fact occur and, if they did, whether they were responsible for the outcomes we had seen.

Finally, we investigated whether certain kinds of students, identifiable at the beginning of the alternative school experience, responded differently to that experience.

We will not go into the technical details of the statistics we employed here. They are available to interested readers from the National Institute of Education. Suffice it to state here that we relied heavily on multiple regressions. We began by using their initial scores to account for the students' attitudes, values, and behaviors at the interim interview, when some students were in an alternative school, and at the final interview when almost all had returned to their conventional schools. Having let the students' initial condition have its effect, so to speak, in predicting the results, we then added the information that some students had attended an alternative school and same had not. That permitted us to tell if school experiences made an additional, independent difference. In doing this, we not only determined the independent effects of schooling, we also made even more comparable the already fairly similar alternative and conventional school groups. Continuing this kind of data analysis, we manipulated the data to find out if certain students responded differently to the alternative programs than others, specifically if students' age, sex, degree of delinquency, and emotional condition at their entry to the program made a difference. When we discovered that students in different emotional states responded differentially to the programs, we separated them out and repeated much of the foregoing analysis on each kind of student separately.

As figure 7 shows, the alternative school students were less disruptive in school at the end of the study than their conventional counterparts. They were not however less delinquent in the community; in fact, they were slightly more delinquent (see fig. 8), although statistical tests tell us that that difference is probably so small as to be within sampling error. The greater reduction found in the disruptive behavior of the alternative students could have occurred by chance only about 6 times in 100 ($p = .06$), while the smaller increase in delinquency in the community has a chance probability level of 38 out of 100 ($p = .38$).

Some explanation of these findings is in order. Although we found that the disruptive and delinquent behavior of the alternative and conventional school students did not differ reliably at the outset of the study, we nevertheless compared their ultimate behavior controlled for whatever differences existed at the outset. So the data we

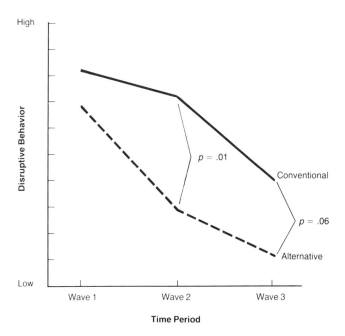

Fig. 7. Changes in disruptive behavior at school for alternative ($n = 46$) and conventional ($n = 43$) school students

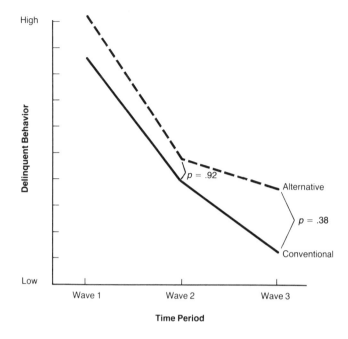

Fig. 8. Changes in delinquent behavior in the community for alternative (n = 59) and conventional (n = 53) school students

have just reported take into account baseline differences at wave 1. The behavioral scores have been "residualized" by the regression techniques briefly described above. We have found that the alternative students are less disruptive, compared to the conventional students, than might have been expected from their behavior at the outset. (We also found them to be less disruptive at wave 3 according to unresidualized scores, but less markedly so—$p < .09$.)

Another point to remember is that these data are based on the reports of the students themselves. Strictly speaking, the data show that the alternative students *reported* being less disruptive at wave 3 than the conventional students did. It is of course conceivable that for some reason the alternative school programs had the effect of changing students' *reporting* behavior and not their actual disruptive and delinquent behavior. But there are several reasons to doubt that this is the case. One reason is that alternative school students did not generally report less problematic behavior: we have seen that they report slightly more delinquent behavior. If only their reporting was changed, it would have to have been an unusually selective effect.

Second, self-reported behavior has proved in many studies to be quite valid. Studies of our own and of other researchers indicate that youth can generally be trusted to report their delinquent behavior honestly and accurately under conditions of confidentiality.

Third, the teachers' ratings of the students' behavior when they returned to the conventional school corroborate the students' reports. We adapted a teachers' rating form employed by D. J. West and David P. Farrington (1973) in London schools, which inquired about behavior such as tardiness, daydreaming, and disobedience. The conventional school teachers, who by and large did not know which if any of their students had been in an alternative school, found the returning alternative school students to be better behaved $(p = .11)$.

Reference to "the returning alternative school students" raises the last point that we want to discuss here. It is possible that the effectiveness of the alternative programs in reducing disruptions at school is spurious. It is conceivable that the finding is a consequence of differential school dropout rates instead. Perhaps the students who went to the alternative schools dropped out of school at a greater rate than their conventional school comparisons did. Especially if the more disruptive of them dropped out selectively, then the alternative students' greater decline in disruptions could have been due to the alternative programs returning only less disruptive students to the conventional schools. This may be said to have eased the burden of the teachers and staff at the conventional schools, just as sending disruptive students to the alternative programs did in the first place, but it would not be valid to conclude that the alternative schools somehow ameliorated the disruptive students' behavior.

However, there is no indication that more disruptive students dropped out selectively. The best measures of how disruptive the dropouts might have been had they remained in school was how disruptive they were at the outset (past behavior is a good predictor of future behavior) and their delinquent behavior in the community after they dropped out (disruptive behavior in school and delinquent behavior in the community are strongly correlated). But dropouts were not reliably different in these respects from those who remained in school.

But the less disruptive behavior of former alternative students may nevertheless be due to selectivity. For we did find a difference

TABLE 9. Disruptive Behavior at School, Comparing Conventional with Alternative Students, Beta, and Other Programs at Wave 3

School	n	Disruptive Behavior Mean[a]	$p_{\text{diff.}}$
Beta			
Alt.	33	−2.61	.08
Conv.	20	2.29	
Other			
Alt.	28	−0.08	.51
Conv.	36	1.18	
Total			
Alt.	61	−1.45	.06
Conv.	56	1.58	

[a] A residualized score, controlling for differences at wave 1 by regression

in retention rates between the alternative and conventional schools. And most of the difference in disruptive behavior at wave 3 seems attributable to the former Beta students (see table 9). While the students who returned to their conventional schools from Alpha and ACE also showed some decline in their disruptive behavior, over and above what might have been expected from their behavior at the outset, it was very slight and statistically unreliable. So differences in the retention rates of the Beta program may be the reason why the alternative students seemed less disruptive at wave 3. But additional findings indicate that this is only partly the reason, if at all.

Social-Psychological Processes of Change

Flexibility of School Rules

The difference between the alternative and conventional schools were quite apparent to the alternative students. According to our data, a pivotal difference was the greater flexibility of the alternative schools' rules and practice, the kind of difference that our theoretical model refers to as personality rather than role regulation. The alternative students found their program markedly more flexible than the conventional students did by the time we interviewed both groups several months after the alternative students had entered the programs (wave 2 interviews). When we asked the alternative students whether there "are any rules that you thought were unfair or unnecessary" in each program, a much larger proportion said "yes" about the conventional school (see table 10). One boy said that the rules regarding dressing for gym class were overly rigid. "If you don't get dressed, you get an E for that day. What if you forgot your gym shoes? How can you get dressed?" Another student objected to rules about tardiness: ". . . one minute late and you get an hour's detention . . . ," and then went on to say, "Some teachers there are like police, always going around checking on things."

Note in table 11 the contrast between those alternative students who were attending conventional school classes concurrently and those who were not. The former were much more favorable about the alternative schools' rules.

At one point in the interview, we presented our respondents with a vignette in which a student tells a teacher, "A group of my friends and I think the rules in this class are stupid," and we asked them in which of four specific ways a teacher at their school was most likely to respond. As table 11 shows, many more of the alternative students expected a sympathetic response even to such a sharp challenge. One of the conventional school students did not think any of our predetermined responses was as likely as the one he offered: "The teacher'll listen to the student's complaints and do nothing. Usually you can't get things changed." Even a conventional school student seemed to be aware of the difference in flexibility between the programs; for she characterized the alternative school students

TABLE 10. Students' Reports of the Fairness of School Rules, Conventional and Alternative School Students Attending One or Both Programs

Q. What do you think of the rules of [school]? Are there any that you think are unfair or unnecessary? (Wave 2)	% "Yes"
Alternative students	
Who attended only one kind of school ($n = 22$)	32
Who attended both programs ($n = 39$)	9
Conventional students ($n = 59$)	71

TABLE 11. Students' Anticipation of Teachers' Responses to a Challenge of School Rules, Conventional and Alternative School Students

Q. In class one day a student stands up and says: "A group of my friends and I think the rules in this class are stupid." Which one of these things is most like what the teacher will do?	Conventional ($n = 65$)	Alternative ($n = 72$)
Tell the students that the rules will not be changed	51%	11%
Send the student to the assistant principal's office	6	1
Listen to the student's complaints and then discuss rules with the whole class	43	88

as, among other things, "the type that can't handle school and the regulations." During the wave 2 interview, 72 percent of the alternative students reported that they were involved in making the rules at their school, compared to 13 percent of the conventional students.

We summed up students' perceptions of the flexibility of school rules in an index composed of intercorrelated items. We found a highly reliable difference ($p < .001$) between the alternative and conventional students' assessments, a difference that proved pivotal in the sense that the process of change in students' attitudes and behavior seemed to depend heavily on the students' perceptions of flexibility.

Flexibility of School Rules and Academic Prospects

Our regression analysis revealed that those students who perceived their schools' rules as being more flexible—whether they were in an alternative or conventional program—gained greater confidence in their academic prospects ($r = .42, p < .001$). Figure 9, the first in a series which will summarize the social-psychological change process as we present it, visualizes this first link in the process. And since the students in the alternative programs clearly regarded their schools' rules as more flexible, several months after they entered the programs they believed that their academic prospects were better than the conventional students did ($p = .006$) (see fig. 10). For example, 93 percent of the conventional alternative students disagreed with the statement, "I don't have much chance of getting passing grades . . ." compared to 77 percent of their conventional counterparts. Only 8 percent of the alternative students said that it was true that "this school treats me like I'm dumb," com-

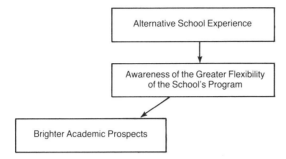

Fig. 9. Model of the social-psychological process of change—flexibility and academic prospects

pared to 26 percent of the conventional students. The greater optimism of the alternative students persisted into the school term after most of them had left the alternative schools, when we interviewed them for the third time ($p < .04$).

But the change in alternative students' feelings about their

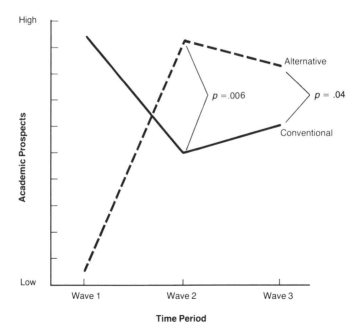

Fig. 10. Changes in academic prospects for alternative ($n = 64$) and conventional ($n = 57$) school students

academic prospects did not follow the same course for all of them, nor did our theory lead us to expect that they would. At this point, we need to make a distinction among the students that will sharpen the findings.

The "Buoyant" and the "Beset"

Earlier we described measures of anxiety and depression that we employed in our interviews. We included these measures because theory and data had led us to believe that our social-psychological model pertained to those youth whose delinquent behavior was mainly provoked by their inadequacies as students. We find that this is true of most heavily delinquent youngsters, but not all. Some youth may be delinquent for other reasons, and an alternative school program would not address their problems. Initial scanning of our data set suggested that this was the case: regression analysis demonstrated that the effects of the alternative schools were conditioned by various signs of anxiety and depression students gave at the outset, during, and at the end of the study.

In order to investigate this phenomenon, we created a summary index of negative affects that our respondents showed during our first interview with them. It is comprised of somatic symptoms of anxiety, the trait anxiety subset of the state-trait anxiety inventory, and the Center for Epidemiological Studies depression scale. Individuals' scores on these three indices are well correlated, in the .40s and .60s, and the summary index is therefore quite coherent, each of the three scales correlating with the total score above .80. We simply summed up the three standardized scores for each individual to assign a total score. Then we arbitrarily divided the students into those in the top third and the bottom two-thirds of the distribution. We call the top third most anxious and depressed students the "beset," and the rest, the "buoyant."

The students who were relatively beset at the time of our first interview with them tended to remain relatively beset throughout the study. The correlations across the three waves of interviews are moderately high and highly reliable (see table 12). It should be pointed out, however, that these correlations do not demonstrate that the "beset" index is a finely discriminating measure of a stable characteristic of individuals. The correlations indicate rather that the index is a fair approximation of a somewhat stable characteristic, and we cannot be certain at this time how discriminating the measure is or how stable the characteristic. But we have found it

TABLE 12. Reliability of the "Beset" Index over
Time, Correlations between Waves 1, 2, and 3 for
Total, Conventional, and Alternative Students

	n	r^a W1 × W2	r^a W2 × W3	r^a W1 × W3
Total	122	.64	.67	.54
Conventional	57	.65	.59	.48
Alternative	55	.64	.74	.57

[a] for all r, $p < .001$

illuminating in this study to characterize the participants according
to their relative positions on the beset index at the outset even while
we are aware that the relative positions of some students shifted as
we observed them over a year and a half.

While the correlations suggest that the alternative students'
scores were slightly more stable from wave 2 to wave 3, the difference between the alternative and conventional students is not
statistically reliable.

The students' scores did not change much over the course of the
study. (See table 13 for interwave differences.) There is some indication ($p = .09$) that the conventional students became more beset
during the first school year. We did find the typical regression effect;
that is, scores tended to converge toward the average over time. The
most beset students at wave 1 became less beset, and the moderately
and least beset—who together comprise the buoyant students—became somewhat more beset. The significant changes occurred between waves 2 and 3.

TABLE 13. Stability of "Beset" Index over Time,
Comparisons of Average Scores in Consecutive Waves
for Total, Conventional, Alternative, and Degrees
of Beset Students

	n	W1	$p_{\text{diff.}}$	W2	$p_{\text{diff.}}$	W3
Total	134	−.02	.86	−.01	.91	−.01
Conventional	61	−.04	.09	.10	.42	.02
Alternative	73	.05	.19	−.06	.30	−.04
Most Beset	46	.96	.001	.55	.65	.49
Moderately Beset	40	−.13	.01	.09	.71	.04
Least Beset	42	−.83	.002	−.61	.27	−.52

The beset youth are of course those who reported to us at the outset that they experienced more than the average frequency of somatic symptoms of anxiety such as headaches and upset stomachs. They felt more tense and nervous. They were more likely to agree that their "life has been a failure" and less likely to agree that "I am hopeful about the future." They said that they more often "feel depressed."

We reported earlier that the alternative students did not differ from their conventional school comparison group on any of the components of the summary index of negative affect. Neither do they differ on the summary index. There was about the same proportion of beset students in the alternative as in the conventional schools. But there are some comparisons between the beset and the buoyant that will be well to keep in mind as we later describe their different responses to their school experiences (see table 14).

The beset and buoyant students are similar in age. A somewhat larger proportion of the beset students are girls. Although this is not a statistically reliable difference in this study, it is consistent with the literature that adolescent girls manifest more symptoms of anxiety and depression than boys do. The beset and the buoyant had

TABLE 14. Comparisons of the Buoyant and the Beset Students at the First Interview

Characteristic	Buoyant[a]	Beset[b]	p_{diff}
% 16 and over	73%	75%	.38
% female	48%	59%	.16
Grade point average	2.99	2.83	.68
Conscious self-esteem (Rosenberg-Bachman)	2.92	2.75	.10
Conscious self-esteem (semantic differential)	5.72	5.26	< .001
Unconscious self-esteem	2.96	2.62	.04
% living with both natural parents	56%	68%	.09
Affection in relationship with father	2.46	1.91	< .001
Affection in relationship with mother	2.74	2.53	.06
"How often would you say you feel that you have no friends you can count on?"			
% "some . . ." or "most of the time"	29%	63%	< .001
"Do you know anyone that really doesn't like you . . . ?"			
% "yes"	43%	57%	.15
Disruptive behavior at school	22.7	25.5	.03
Delinquent behavior in the community	31.7	37.2	.04

[a] n varies from 89 (relationship with father) to 117
[b] n varies from 50 (relationship with father) to 63

about the same low grade point average in the term before some of them entered an alternative program.

The self-esteem of the beset was expectedly lower, whether measured by transparent items that tap conscious levels of awareness or by the projective test of unconscious self-esteem.

A greater proportion of the beset lived with both natural parents, but their relationships with their parents, especially with their father, was markedly poorer. They also felt more often that they could not count on their friends, and a majority of them believed that there was someone who didn't like them and would harm them if he could.

The beset admitted to more disruptive behavior at school and to more delinquent behavior in the community than the more buoyant students did at the outset.

In several respects, then, their relative scores fill out the image of the anxious and depressed, beset students. That they also behaved worse than the buoyant youngsters has two implications. First, this finding is contrary to our theoretical image of them; we expected that delinquent behavior would effectively defend youngsters from negative affects. Apparently we have here a highly delinquent set who were nevertheless beset. They resemble the unsocialized "neurotic" type of delinquent that Hewitt and Jenkins (1947) identified from clinical records. Second, the level of their misbehavior makes them priority targets for change. But if they are indeed a different type of delinquent, then our theory suggests—and the data confirm—that a school-based program is not so likely to have much effect on them.

Differential Response of Buoyant and Beset Students to Their Schools' Flexibility

During the school year in which they attended the alternative schools, both buoyant and beset students were more optimistic about their academic prospects than their conventional school counterparts (see figs. 11 and 12). Actually, the beset alternative students were relatively more optimistic than their buoyant classmates, since their beset counterparts at the conventional schools were so pessimistic. But the relative optimism of the beset did not last through the school year after they left the alternative program; by that time, they were only slightly and statistically unreliably ($p = .41$) more optimistic than the beset students who had had no alternative experience. On the other hand, the buoyant former alternative students remained reliably ($p = .04$) more optimistic.

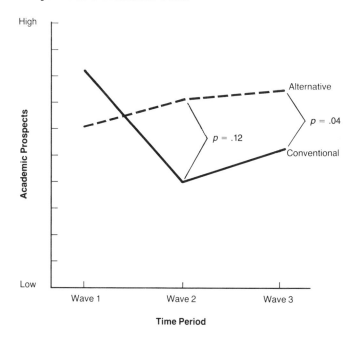

Fig. 11. Changes in academic prospects for *buoyant* alternative ($n = 44$) and conventional ($n = 39$) school students

Apparently, for the conventional and alternative beset students, the flexibility of their schools was not as determinative of their academic prospects as it was among the buoyant students. As the correlations in table 15 show, school flexibility and academic prospects are related consistently less well among the beset compared to the buoyant. Indeed, in three out of four instances, the correlations for the beset are actually negative. So the perceptions of the beset alternative students that their schools were more flexible did not contribute to their optimism about academic success. Not only did the academic prospects of the beset alternative students fade over time, but they also seemed ultimately unrelated to the beset students' problematic behavior. The academic prospects of the beset students with alternative school experience were at wave 3 unreliably correlated with their disruptive behavior at school ($r = .13, p > .10$) and with their delinquent behavior in the community ($r = .12, p > .10$). This was true of the beset conventional students as well ($r = .10, p > .10, r = .16, p > .10$). Note that these correlations are all positive, not reliably different from zero but

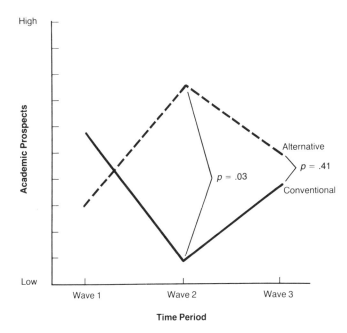

Fig. 12. Changes in academic prospects for *beset* alternative (*n* = 20) and conventional (*n* = 18) school students

showing that, if anything, the *more* optimistic the students, the *more* disruptive and delinquent they tended to be. In contrast, the buoyant students' academic prospects were inversely correlated with their problematic behavior: among the former alternative stu-

TABLE 15. Relationships between School Flexibility and Academic Prospects for Conventional and Alternative Buoyant and Beset Students at Waves 2 and 3

	Wave 2				Wave 3			
	r	*n*	*p*	p_{diff}	*r*	*n*	*p*	p_{diff}
Conventional								
Buoyant	.15	39	.36	.22	.29	39	.07	.34
Beset	−.22	18	.39		−.01	18	.95	
Alternative								
Buoyant	.63	44	< .001	.20	.22	42	.16	.22
Beset	.37	19	.12		−.12	20	.63	

dents, the correlations are $-.40$ ($p < .05$) for disruptive behavior in
school and $-.11$ ($p > .10$) for delinquent behavior in the community;
and among the conventional students, $-.33$ ($p < .05$), and $-.22$ ($p > .10$) respectively.

Since the alternative school experience effected change in their
students' behavior partly by raising their academic prospects, the
facts that the beset students' optimism did not remain high and was
not finally related to their behavior are reasons that the alternative
schools were not as effective with them. We will return to this point
after exploring other facets of the social-psychological changes. Figure 9 presents the model of change we have just discussed, but the
reader should keep in mind from this point forward that the model
fits only those students who were more buoyant at the outset.

Flexibility of School Rules and Commitment to the Role of the Student

Our regression analysis showed that students who at wave 2
perceived their schools as being more flexible—whether they were
alternative or conventional school students—were more committed
to the role of student ($p < .001$). Optimism about their brighter
academic prospects was also related to greater commitment to the
role of student ($r = .28$, $p < .01$). Indeed, during the time students
were in the alternative schools—that is, at the second wave of interviews—the alternative schools' greater flexibility seemed to affect
their students' greater commitment to the role largely indirectly by
raising their academic prospects rather than directly. Only later, at
wave 3, was the perceived flexibility of the alternative schools' programs that they had attended itself a significant contributor to students' role commitment.

Since more of the alternative students believed that their
schools' rules were more flexible, they became on the average more
committed to studenthood in the alternative programs: they felt
they were working closer to their capacity, putting in more effort,
and were more satisfied with their performances ($p < .03$). One boy
had just come into the alternative program from a special program
for slow learners when we asked him if he would go to school if he
didn't have to. He chose among the predetermined responses "definitely not" and explained, "School don't turn me on too much." But
he had changed his mind to "probably yes" after some months in the
alternative program "'Cause there'd be nothin' else to do." At wave
3, after he had returned to, then dropped out of the conventional
school, he again responded "Definitely not . . . because I never liked

school. Well, I liked it in the sixth grade. But I went mostly to see the chicks. I wanted to get an education but not if they hassled me." An alternative school girl thought she would probably go to school because "Alpha—I really like it there—not so much the coffee and sitting around . . . the teachers really understand." Even among that majority of conventional school students who thought they would probably go to school even if they did not have to, some were clearly not enthusiastic about their school itself. One answered that he wanted "to get my education. It's not how I really feel right now though about school." Another conventional student said that "An independent education may be better . . . Get more personal contact doing library research. Or maybe go to [a private academy]."

Just being in one of the alternative schools itself, regardless of their perceptions of the schools' flexibility, also encouraged students' commitment to the role, but to a lesser degree after those first months ($p < .07$). But when, at wave 3, almost all of the students had left the alternative school, then the more alternative school experience the students had had, the more committed they were to the student role ($p = .001$), and their perceptions of the flexibility of their current school's rules did not make so much difference ($p = .16$). So at our last interview with them, the alternative school students exhibited substantially greater commitment to the student role ($p < .001$).

While enough of the alternative students became more committed to the student role after several months in the program so that the alternative group as a whole differed in this respect from the conventional comparison group, the greater commitment was almost entirely by buoyant youth. As figures 13 and 14 show, the buoyant alternative students expressed substantially greater commitment at wave 2 than the buoyant conventional students did ($p < .001$); but the difference among the beset students was quite small and statistically unreliable ($p = .93$). This was partly because the beset students' commitment to being students was not so strongly encouraged by the flexibility of their schools. The correlation between their perceptions of flexibility and their commitment is insignificantly negative ($r = -.03$), while the correlation for the buoyant alternative students is reliably positive ($r = .31, p = .10$). In the middle of the following school year, the buoyant students who had attended an alternative school remained more committed to being students than their buoyant peers who had attended only conventional schools ($p < .001$). But the beset, former alternative students were only slightly and unreliably more committed than

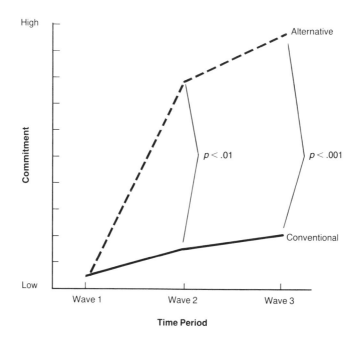

Fig. 13. Changes in commitment to the student role for *buoyant* alternative ($n = 37$) and conventional ($n = 35$) school students

their conventional counterparts ($p = .13$). Figure 15 summarizes the discussion up to now of the process of change as the buoyant alternative students experienced it.

Academic Prospects, Commitment to the Student Role, and Attitude toward School

Continuing our discussion of the social psychological process of change, we now consider the students' general attitude toward school. Most of the differential effects of the alternative and conventional schools on disruptive and delinquent behavior were mediated by the students' general attitude toward school. Shaped by students' beliefs in their academic prospects and by their commitment to the role of student, it was ultimately an important determinant of the students' behavior.

We have already described how we measured students' attitude toward school. Its components are a global expression of liking school, a positive feeling for teachers, participation in extracurricular activities, and one's usual mood at the end of the school day.

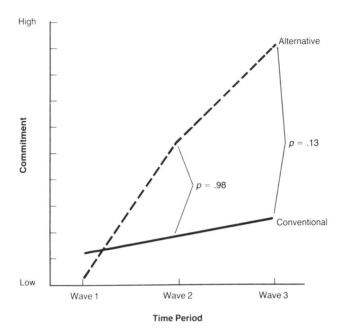

Fig. 14. Changes in commitment to the student role for *beset* alternative (*n* = 14) and conventional (*n* = 17) school students

A change in students' attitudes toward school depended heavily on changes in their academic prospects and in their commitment to the student role. Not surprisingly, when these changes did not occur, students' attitudes toward school were not likely to change. We have already seen that the alternative school students were

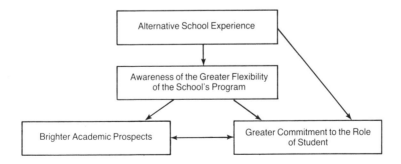

Fig. 15. Model of social-psychological process of change — flexibility, academic prospects, and commitment to the role of student

more negative toward their conventional school at the outset than the comparison students who remained in the conventional school. This difference may have been generated by the selection of the more negative students for referral to the alternative program, but we believe it more likely that it was generated by the alternative students' comparing their new program with their old after only a brief experience with the former. In any case, after several months the alternative students were no longer so down on school. By wave 2, they expressed markedly more positive attitudes ($p < .001$) than their conventional school counterparts did. Of course, the alternative school students were at that time expressing their opinions about their alternative school.

One boy who had at the outset told our interviewer that he was "mostly bored" with school, at wave 2 rejected the vignette we offered him about a student announcing to his teacher that school "is a bore." "This wouldn't really happen at Beta," he said, "because we have a choice of what we do in seminar." He said that he liked Beta on account of the contract system. "You can work at your own pace."

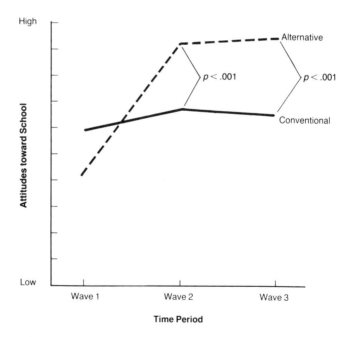

Fig. 16. Changes in attitudes toward school for *buoyant* alternative ($n = 39$) and conventional ($n = 35$) school students

He boasted to his interviewer that he and only one other student in his class had earned extra credit for their work in the Beta seminar, and he mentioned this again at our third interview with him.

A girl who at the second interview was taking classes at Alpha and at a conventional school compared them. "[Alpha] is a lot better way of schooling. You get more out of the class." Another boy reflected on his conventional school experience: "It wasn't like Alpha. No one cared at _____."

Meanwhile, it was more typical of the conventional school students to complain. As one boy said, "I don't like the schools, and I know a lot of people who don't like them."

Both the buoyant and the beset alternative students were reliably more positive toward school at wave 2 ($p < .001, p < .02$) than their conventional school comparisons were, but the difference was somewhat greater among the buoyant ones (see figs. 16 and 17). However, by the time most of the students had left the alternative school, at wave 3, only the buoyant former alternative students maintained the difference ($p < .001$). The beset students were still

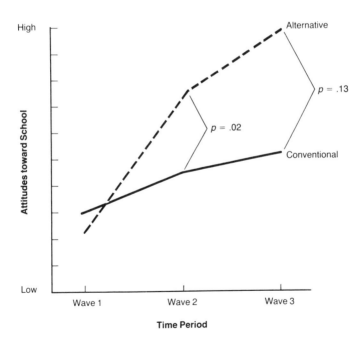

Fig. 17. Changes in attitudes toward school for *beset* alternative ($n = 14$) and conventional ($n = 16$) school students

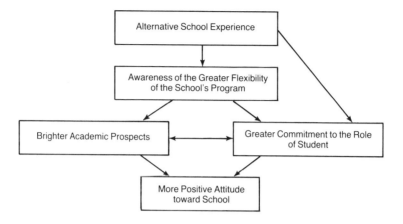

Fig. 18. Model of the social-psychological process of change—attitudes toward school

somewhat more positive if they had had some alternative school experience, but not reliably so ($p = .13$). That the attitudes toward school of the beset alternative students no longer differed reliably from the beset conventional students is due partly of course to the fact that they no longer differed on two important conditions for positive attitudes, optimism about their academic prospects and commitment to the role of student (see fig. 18). An additional reason might be that these two factors at wave 3 related less strongly to beset students' feelings about school. Their correlations were in the .20s, unreliably lower than all the other sets of students whose correlations ranged from the .30s to the .50s.

TABLE 16. Correlations between Attitude toward School and Disruptive Behavior for Conventional and Alternative Buoyant and Beset Students at Wave 3

	n	r	p	p_{diff}
Buoyant				
Conventional	40	−.48	< .01	ns
Alternative	38	−.40	< .05	
Beset				
Conventional	17	−.43	< .10	.004
Alternative	25	.32	< .20	

Attitude toward School and Disruptive Behavior

As one might expect, students' attitude toward school was a substantial determinant of how disruptive of school they were (see table 16 for the correlations). Inasmuch as the attitudes of the buoyant alternative students improved markedly, their disruptive behavior declined. But the fact that the beset alternative students had no more positive attitudes than the beset conventional students helps to explain why, by wave 3, they were no less disruptive (see figs. 19 and 20). But that is only partly the reason. Strangely enough, at wave 3, the attitudes of the beset students toward school were *not* negatively related to their disruptive behavior; quite to the contrary, the more positive the beset alternative students were, the more disruptive they were. We hesitate to attribute this unexpected relationship to some general irrationality of beset students, for the beset conventional students did not exhibit it; the relationship is reliably more positive among the alternative beset ($p = .004$). If the finding is real—and sometimes data display such oddities by chance, even if improbably—then it seems to have something to do with the beset students' alternative school experience.

We considered the possibility that the alternative school further upset the already beset students. They were as aware as their buoyant classmates that their alternative schools were more flexible, ready to meet them more than halfway so that they might succeed as students. Nevertheless, the psychological state in which they entered the programs, or perhaps something else, prevented them from taking advantage of the program and they did no better scholastically. We thought that this may have generated even greater frustration and contributed to their continuing disruptive behavior. In order to check this possibility, we looked at our data to see if the beset alternative students showed any indications that they blamed themselves for scholastic failure more than the other youth did. We had asked all the participants whether, if they found themselves doing poorly in school, it would more likely be attributable to "being unlucky," to "difficult work," to lack of effort or to lack of ability. The modal attribution of all the students was to their lack of effort, but during the third interview, 72 percent of the buoyant students gave this reason, compared to 55 percent of the beset. The beset alternative students were not more likely to blame themselves than the other students were. If anything, more of them and of their beset comparison group blamed the difficulty of the work and their unlucky fate.

Nor did the beset alternative students come to think of themselves as less intelligent than their peers. At wave 3, we asked students whether they thought that they were "not quite as intelligent as . . .", "as intelligent as . . .", or "maybe more intelligent than . . . most others your age." Most of them felt that they were of average intelligence, and the beset alternative students did not differ in this regard.

We wondered if their positive attitudes toward school did not ameliorate the beset alternative students' disruptive behavior because they felt that their alternative school referral had somehow stigmatized them. We have already seen that their optimism about their academic prospects did not last, as their buoyant classmates' had, after they had left the alternative programs. In order to assess the alternative students' feelings of stigma, we asked them whether there was anyone who they'd rather did not know that they had attended an alternative school. Only 14 percent said yes, and no larger proportion of beset students did than buoyant ones.

In short, we do not really understand why more positive attitudes toward school were not related to less disruptive behavior among the beset alternative students, as they were among the other

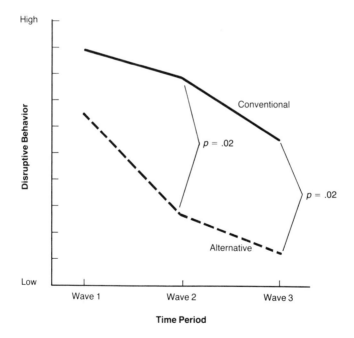

Fig. 19. Changes in disruptive behavior at school for *buoyant* alternative ($n = 29$) and conventional ($n = 31$) school students

students. This is for us the most curious part of the general pattern, that the special nature of the alternative schools consistently failed for their beset students to call into play social psychological processes that led to less disruptive behavior. We have speculated that the beset students' problems lay largely elsewhere than in school, and that their poor scholastic performance, as their disruptive and delinquent behavior, is a consequence of those problems. But that does not explain why the relationship between attitudes and behavior among the beset alternative students differed in our study from the relationship among the beset conventional students. At this point, a plausible explanation awaits more theory and further research.

At any rate, the relatively better behavior of the buoyant former alternative school students was confirmed by their teachers. We reported earlier that the teachers in the conventional school, without being aware of which of their current students had attended an alternative school, rated those students' behavior as better than their conventional school classmates. Now we find that this difference was entirely among the buoyant students ($p = .02$); the

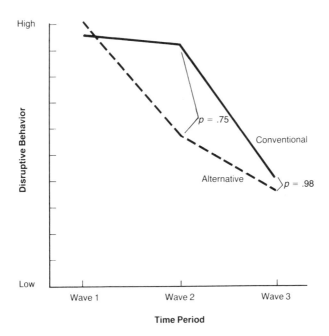

Fig. 20. Changes in disruptive behavior at school for *beset* alternative ($n = 17$) and conventional ($n = 12$) school students

teachers did not report any reliable difference among the beset students ($p = .69$).

Disruptive Behavior in School and Delinquent Behavior in the Community

Figure 21 summarizes the whole social psychological process of change, from school experiences through their effects on delinquent behavior in the community, as we found it among the buoyant students. It can be seen that, not surprisingly, to the degree that youngsters' behavior in school improved, their behavior in the community improved as well. The two sets of behavior are highly correlated, about equally among the buoyant and beset students.

Even though the disruptive school behavior of the buoyant alternative students declined significantly more by the third interview than that of their conventional counterparts had, their delinquent behavior in the community did not, notwithstanding the correlation between the two sets of behaviors. It appears that midway

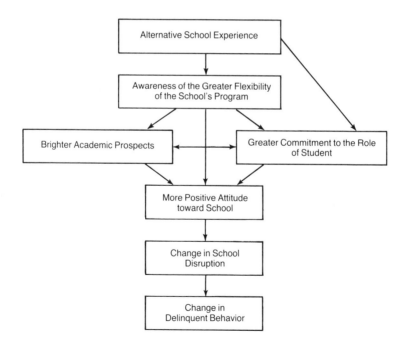

Fig. 21. Model of the social-psychological process of change—disruptive and delinquent behavior

through the school year after their alternative experience, the alternative experience had not yet had an effect on the way buoyant students were behaving outside of school. While their delinquent behavior had declined somewhat since our initial interview with them, it declined no more than the delinquency of the buoyant conventional students did. It is quite possible that their delinquent behavior lessened later, and that a follow-up study will discover that. For as we have seen, several of their school-related attitudes and behaviors changed in ways conducive to less delinquency.

The delinquent behavior of the beset alternative students also declined over the course of the study, but not quite as much as their buoyant classmates' did (see figs. 22 and 23). From one school year to the next, the delinquency of the buoyant alternative students declined by 12 percent, and of the beset students, by 6 percent. (The comparable figures among the conventional students are 11 and 15 percent.) The smaller decline among the beset alternative students, while not statistically reliable, is consistent with the other data which suggest that, if anything, the alternative experience affected them negatively.

We were unable to determine if official records of delinquency compiled by the local police and courts matched our findings from the self-report of students. So few of the participants in the study were arrested by the police while we were observing them that we could not analyze these data.

The Model in the Separate Programs

Separate analyses like those just reported were done for each of the three alternative programs and their respective comparison groups. The numbers of students in each program are small for statistical analyses, so that only very large differences are reliable at conventionally acceptable probability levels. This is especially true when data are analyzed separately for the buoyant and beset children at each of the alternative and conventional schools. Furthermore, comparing one alternative school directly with another in this study is not legitimate because the three programs did not select their students from the same pool. So Alpha, Beta, and ACE may have recruited students who, to begin with, were differentially ready for change. Any comparison among the alternative programs must be limited to the differences they made relative to their own comparison group.

Table 17 presents data showing the effects of each alternative school on school grades, disruptive behavior in school, and delinquent behavior in the community. The averages in table 17 are for wave 3, adjusted by regression for the baseline measures of the three levels of outcomes taken at the first interview. Few of the differences between the alternative and conventional schools are statistically reliable, but their tendencies generally parallel the findings for the three programs taken together: the school grades of buoyant former alternative school students were higher than those of the conventional students, their disruptive behavior was lower, and delinquent behavior was slightly higher; the differences among the beset students were not as great or as consistent in direction.

There are some other features of the outcome data for the separate programs that are worth noting, with caution because of their unreliability. Beta may have had a more positive effect on beset students than either Alpha or ACE did: its beset students' grades and behavior in and out of school all improved relative to the comparison group. ACE on the other hand does not seem to have reduced disruptive behavior among its buoyant students as much as

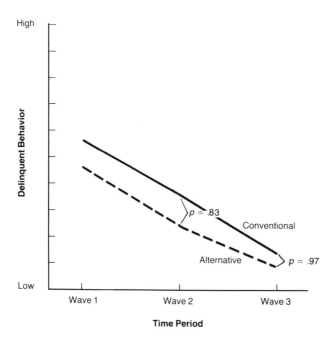

Fig. 22. Changes in delinquent behavior in the community for *buoyant* alternative (*n* = 29) and conventional (*n* = 37) school students

Alpha and Beta did: these students' adjusted scores for disruption were at wave 3 even slightly higher than the comparable conventional students'.

Insofar as these data can be trusted, of the three programs, Alpha seemed to have had the most marked effects on its students' grades and disruptive behavior in school. Alpha's buoyant students reported more improvement at the third interview and its beset students reported more deterioration relative to their comparison groups. This impression is reinforced by the fact that the components of the theoretical model seem more closely tied together empirically in the Alpha data. If one follows various paths through the change process, starting from the alternative school experience and ending with disruptive behavior at school, compounding the probabilities that one change will lead to the next, the probability that disruptive behavior will decline as a consequence of attending Alpha is at least two times greater than if students attended ACE or Beta. Why this might have occurred is worth discussing because it

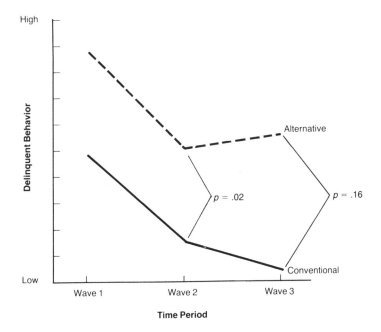

Fig. 23. Changes in delinquent behavior in the community for *beset* alternative ($n = 20$) and conventional ($n = 16$) school students

may set some priorities for alternative school practices and suggest theoretical refinements.

Distinctive about Alpha, according to our data, was that its students' attitudes toward school were not so crucial for the level of their disruptive behavior when they returned to the conventional schools. Instead, Alpha's effect on behavior was more directly attributable to its students' commitment to the role of student at that time. Actually, they had not become markedly more committed while they were attending Alpha. The role that they played in Alpha's more group-therapeutic modality hardly resembled that of student. But perhaps Alpha's buoyant students gained through their discussions and through their journals some understanding about themselves and about schooling that enabled them ultimately to play the conventional student role more effectively. And perhaps

TABLE 17. Differences in the Effects of the Conventional and Alternative Schools for Buoyant and Beset Students Separately for the Three Alternative Programs

	School Grades			Disruptive Behavior in School			Delinquent Behavior in the Community		
		n	p		n	p		n	p
Alpha									
Buoyant									
Conventional	−.26	16		.37	9		−.16	16	
Alternative	.38	9	.08	−.49	10	.05	−.18	14	.97
Beset									
Conventional	−.21	4		−.41	3		−.23	4	
Alternative	−.11	5	.89	.42	5	.13	.84	7	.08
Beta									
Buoyant									
Conventional	−.04	14		.34	12		.30	13	
Alternative	.29	16	.32	−.21	18	.14	.10	24	.70
Beset									
Conventional	−.09	9		.06	8		−.24	10	
Alternative	.32	10	.38	−.32	15	.38	−.11	10	.77
ACE									
Buoyant									
Conventional	−.44	19		.14	18		−.13	18	
Alternative	.40	10	.16	.20	8	.81	−.05	8	.88
Beset									
Conventional	.20	5		−.05	6		−.32	7	
Alternative	.05	3	.61	.19	5	.60	−.55	5	.34

the beset students' experience at Alpha proved to be too introspective and probing for them, since they seemed already too conscious of their anxiety and depression.

In contrast, the effect of ACE was almost entirely mediated by its students' attitudes toward school. As long as these attitudes remained positive, their behavior was more tolerable. But when they finally returned to the conventional school, their attitudes toward school became more negative and did not sustain change in the students' behavior. And ACE's students did not seem to have reformulated their orientation to the role of student independent of their feelings about schools generally.

The process of change was most loosely integrated at Beta. The empirical paths from the Beta experience to ultimately better behavior at school summed up to the lowest probability that the former would lead to the latter. Probably this was due to the organizational and recruitment problems that developed at Beta during the period that we observed the program. Beta students may not have been convinced that what happened at Beta had much to do with their ability to cope with the conventional system. Clearly Beta students did not become more optimistic about their academic prospects as a result of their successes as Beta students; rather, while they were at Beta, their optimism declined relative to the conventional comparison group. What effect Beta had seems due largely to the way its human relations seminar and the flexible image of the program encouraged its students to commit themselves to the role of student and improved students' attitudes toward school. That Beta was perhaps more effective with its beset students than Alpha or ACE were may have been due to the practical training in coping that was given in Beta's human relations seminar; it was less scholastic than ACE's curriculum and forced less introspection than Alpha's workshops—and may have been less threatening to beset students on both counts.

The reader will recall that it seemed from the preliminary stages of our data analyses that the Beta program had the strongest overall effect on its students, and that this may have been spurious, due, at least in part, to selective dropping out by Beta's most troublesome students. Further analysis has shown, however, that the stronger overall effect of Beta was due to its more positive effect on its beset students. Actually, the alternative schools as a whole had their most positive effects on their buoyant students, and Alpha was the most effective of the three in this regard. And Alpha's effects cannot be explained by selective dropping out. The effect seems attributable rather to the social-psychological processes that we have described.

Effect on School Grades

While we undertook this study to determine if a particular kind of alternative school would have any effect on adolescents' disruptive and delinquent behavior, some educators have argued that delinquent behavior in the community is after all not the schools' responsibility. School programs, the argument goes, ought not be evaluated with reduced delinquent behavior as a criterion. The schools' job, according to this view, is to improve students' skills and to maintain sufficiently ordered behavior at school so that students may attend to their studies. Thus, our finding that the alternative schools effected a significant reduction in the disruptive behavior of their more buoyant students is a gratifying result even while the alternative schools had no marked effect on delinquency.

It is also true that the alternative schools seemed to have had a

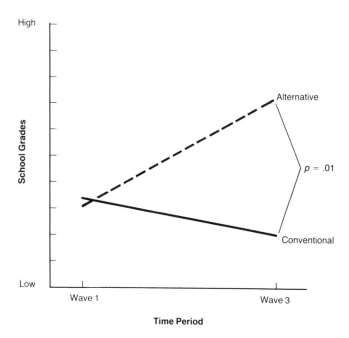

Fig. 24. Change in school grades for *buoyant* alternative (*n* = 35) and conventional (*n* = 49) school students

positive effect on the grades their buoyant students earned when they returned to the conventional schools. When students were first entering the alternative programs, their grades did not differ from the students who remained in the conventional schools. But as figures 24 and 25 show, those buoyant alternative students who returned to conventional schools a year later (some had been taking some classes there all along) received reliably higher grades (p = .009). The grades of beset alternative students also went up slightly, as did the grades of their conventional counterparts, and there was no reliable difference in these two groups' grades at wave 3 (p = .76).

We also measured the scholastic skills of students independently of teachers' grades. We did this at the urging of the funding agency, the National Institute of Education (NIE). NIE felt that teachers might not be objective in their grading of students who had a reputation for being troublesome and might be especially biased about students who had attended an alternative program. We did not have enough time during our interviews with students to mea-

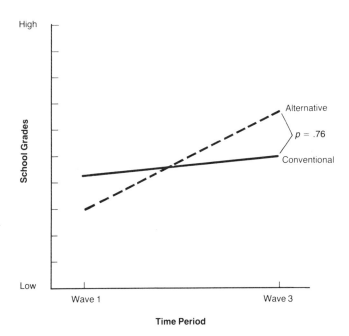

Fig. 25. Change in school grades for *beset* alternative (n = 18) and conventional (n = 18) school students

sure scholastic skills extensively. We used a subtest of the Wide Range Achievement Test (WRAT) in which respondents attempted to read aloud a series of seventy-four words of increasing difficulty. Level of ability is gauged by the point at which respondents make ten consecutive errors.

Perhaps a more thorough measure would have detected a gain in skills that matched students' improvements in grades. But our analyses of WRAT scores found no reliable differences among students, conventional and alternative, buoyant and beset, at the outset or at the end of the study.

At this point, we should raise two questions about whether it is valid to attribute the better grades of the alternative students to their experience in the alternative program. First, it might be due instead to a positive bias on the part of teachers. But this explanation is ruled out by the fact that the conventional school teachers were not able, toward the end of the following year, to identify students who had attended an alternative program. During the course of collecting their ratings of students' behavior, we asked teachers to identify any students on the list who had attended any special program in the recent past. We found that almost none of the alternative students—less than 5 percent—were known to have been such.

The second issue is a wider one, one that we touched upon earlier. Remember that more of the buoyant alternative students had dropped out of school during the course of the study. It is plausible that those who dropped out had been the poorer students to begin with, and that the superior scholastic performance of the buoyant alternative students at wave 3 was a consequence of selection: the poorer students in the category were no longer in school. But actually that is not the case. As table 18 shows, the buoyant alternative students who ultimately dropped out of school were not the poorer students; their grades before they entered the alternative school were not reliably different from their buoyant classmates, and in fact were slightly better. So it is doubtful that selection can explain the better grades of the buoyant alternative students afterward. It is more likely that this was an effect of the alternative program.

Note in table 18 that the beset conventional students who remained in school had earned the highest grades of all. But even taking the poorer initial grades of the beset alternative students into account does not alter the finding that they performed no better scholastically at wave 3 than their comparison group did.

**TABLE 18. Comparison between Dropouts'
and Others' Grades at Wave 1 within Groups
of Conventional and Alternative Buoyant and Beset
Students**

	Dropouts		Others[a]		
		n		n	p_{diff}
Conventional					
Buoyant	3.03	7	2.91	42	.69
Beset	2.50	6	3.22	16	.15
Alternative					
Buoyant	3.02	18	2.89	30	.65
Beset	2.38	10	2.96	17	.12

[a] Includes graduates and current students

We had earlier considered the possibility that selective dropping out of school might explain the less disruptive behavior at wave 3 of the buoyant alternative compared to the buoyant conventional students. It may have been that the effect of the alternative programs was simply to have eased the poorer and more disruptive students out of school. We cannot completely disregard the explanation of selection, but the pattern of the data suggests that it is not all, if any, of the explanation for the findings. For it is clear that the social-psychological processes associated with better behavior and better performance—greater flexibility of the school program, greater optimism about one's academic prospects, more positive attitudes toward school—occurred to a significantly greater degree among the students, especially the buoyant students, in the alternative schools. It seems to us quite probable that the alternative schools produced, in part or whole, the positive effects the data demonstrate.

We would be even more certain about this conclusion if the buoyant alternative students also exhibited significantly less delinquent behavior in the community at the time of our third interview with them. Of course, this outcome would not have been directly affected by students dropping out of school. On the other hand, there would still have been some doubt about attributing even this result to the beneficial effects of the alternative schools, because it has been shown in other studies (Elliott 1966; Elliott and Voss 1974) that the delinquent behavior of school dropouts declines relative to those who remain in school!

In our concluding chapter, we will discuss how further research and improved alternative programs can together help resolve with more certainty the question of what is the explanation for the positive outcomes that these data document.

Potential Conditions of Change

Stigma

One of the potentially negative aspects of an alternative school experience is stigmatization. Youngsters may be made to feel that they are different in a derogatory sense by having been sent to a special school. It is for this reason that "mainstreaming" children with all sorts of impairments—physical, intellectual, and emotional—is now being mandated by law and educational policy to an increasing extent.

We have already described the negative opinions of the alternative programs that were held by a substantial number of conventional school teachers and staff members. It is also clear from our interviews that many students also derogated the alternative schools and the youngsters who had to go there. One girl tried to be kind when we asked her to describe the "kids your age in [the alternative schools associated with her high school]": "They're not as fortunate," she said. "We're in the high school with everybody and they're off by themselves with just a few people. . . . They have problems at home, and they're just not getting along. . . . They needed special attention for themselves, like a teacher to talk just with them alone. They didn't do good in the regular high school." A boy thought, "They're lucky to get into it, because I tried to and I couldn't. . . . They're not smart enough for the regular school and they're trying to get out of the work because that's easier." Others were distinctly negative: "They're lazy. That's just a school for people who don't want to do it"; "Seems like most of them are slow—not slow, they don't want to try"; "They need some growing up."

And the alternative school students were probably aware of others' opinions of them and their school. One girl reported that her art teacher and she did not get along because the teacher "is down on Alpha." Another told us that she didn't want some of the kids in her neighborhood or their parents to know that she was attending an alternative school: "Some people think Alpha is just for dumb people, but it's really not. Alpha's there so you can go and get some credits and learn about yourself." Other alternative students agreed with the negative image of their classmates. A boy said: "A lot of them have problems and are slow and all that. . . . But they're nice people. . . . They just get into a little bit of trouble." Another boy initially described his alternative classmates with the same term as he described his former classmates in the high school: "Brats." After he had attended the alternative school for several months, he had changed his mind: the conventional school students were still "brats," but his classmates at ACE, "They're OK." By our third interview with them, the students who had had alternative experience were almost invariably positive about their former classmates: "They're no different. I like them"; "They're decent . . . pretty cool"; "Really nice people"; "They're all trying to learn. I did better in that school than in any other school." For the most part, alternative students did not continue to feel stigmatized. During our third interview with them, only 14 percent said they'd prefer that certain people not know that they had attended an alternative school.

Since so few of their students felt thus stigmatized, it is not possible to determine in our data whether stigma interfered with efforts of the alternative schools. The programs in this study did not seem affected by it. So we can conclude that alternative programs may be effective even though they may be negatively regarded by the teachers and students in the conventional schools. The alternative students may develop their own positive feelings out of their own experiences.

Initial Degrees of Misbehavior of Students and Their Friends

Here we address the question of whether the effect of the alternative schools was conditional on the troublesomeness of the students they enrolled. Alternative schools would make a greater contribution to their communities' welfare if they were at least as effective with their more as with their less delinquent and disruptive students. In order to investigate this, we analyzed our data separately for students who initially confessed to above and below average amounts of misbehavior in school and in the community.

At the same time, we also took into account the misbehavior of the students' friends because it is related closely to students' own misbehavior. Indeed, a common explanation for a particular youngster becoming heavily disruptive and delinquent is that he or she got into the wrong crowd. This explanation is often given by this youngster's parents. It is comforting for the parents of seriously delinquent youth to have something beside themselves to blame; and many of them are genuinely puzzled by their children's behavior because they did not bring them up that way. Blaming peer associates finds support in theories of delinquency that identify variously the "gang," the "delinquent subculture," and "differential association with criminal elements" as major causes of delinquency; and in the data which show that heavily delinquent youth typically have heavily delinquent friends and usually commit delinquent acts in their company.

Our own view assigns companions only minor weight as a cause of delinquency. Our reading of the literature suggests that having heavily delinquent friends is a consequence more than a cause of a youngster's propensity to be delinquent. We believe that youth who are provoked to be delinquent search out an appreciative audience for their performance from among their peers. Their having delinquent friends is a matter of choice. Peers facilitate delinquent behavior; they are a prime audience for delinquent performances; but they are not a major impetus to delinquency.

In this study, we asked students to estimate the degree of their friends' delinquency. We wanted to see if having more or less delinquent friends made a difference in the effect of the alternative schools. Did having more delinquent friends impede the efforts of the schools? Was changing their students' peer associates one way in which the alternative schools accomplished their goals? So we asked respondents, "Of ten of your friends, how many have . . . ?" and presented them with the same list of delinquent and disruptive behaviors that we used to elicit confessions of their own misbehavior.

These data demonstrate the typical high correlations between youngsters' self-reported delinquency and their estimates of their friends' delinquency, correlations ranging from .48 to .70, and highly reliable ($p < .001$). The buoyant and beset participants showed equally strong correlations. The correlations were as strong at the beginning as at the end of the study. Consistent with the data that showed that the beset students themselves were somewhat more delinquent throughout the study than their buoyant classmates, they also reported that their friends were more delinquent.

Our data indicate that the positive effect of the alternative schools was more marked among the buoyant students who were more disruptive than average when they entered the program. While the disruptive behavior of the initially less disruptive buoyant students also declined, the decline among the more disruptive is statistically more reliable ($p = .06$ compared to $p = .21$). The initial level of misbehavior of the beset students made no difference; neither the more nor less disruptive and delinquent students evidenced any reliable change relative to their conventional counterparts.

Analyses of the data on the misbehavior of the students' friends generated parallel findings, which is not surprising since students' own misbehavior and that of their friends are so closely related. The programs were more effective in reducing the disruptive behavior of buoyant students who initially reported their friends' disruptiveness to be higher than average. In fact, this finding is more reliable ($p = .01$) than the one involving the initial level of students' own disruptiveness. Was this because the effect of the alternative schools was at least in part due to changes in their students' companions?

Actually, the effect of the alternative schools does not seem to have been mediated by changes in the disruptive or delinquent behavior of their students' friends. At wave 3, the buoyant alternative students' estimates of their friends' disruptive and delinquent behavior were no lower than the buoyant conventional students' estimates, although, as we have seen, the disruptive behavior of the former had declined more than that of the latter. Similarly, the estimates of the alternative beset students, higher to begin with, remained higher than the beset conventional students' throughout the study, as their own delinquent behavior did. The alternative schools had no apparent marked effect on the behavior of their students' companions.

When their estimates of their friends' disruptive and delinquent behaviors are joined in regression equations with their attitudes toward school as predictors to their own misbehavior, buoyant students' attitudes toward school persist as reliable predictors to their disruptive behavior at school. But, as we have seen in similar analyses, beset students' attitudes toward school are unreliable predictors to their disruptive behavior.

In sum, it appears that the positive effects of the alternative schools on their buoyant students was more marked, perhaps even limited to those who had been more disruptive when they first entered the programs. The alternative schools had no marked effect on their beset students, no matter what their initial level of misbehavior. (And the reader should recall here that the beset students were at the outset somewhat more delinquent and disruptive than their buoyant classmates.)

Buoyant students' initial estimates of their friends' misbehavior also distinguishes those with whom the program was more and less successful, perhaps even better than the students' own initial confessions do. But this was not due to the programs' affecting the misbehavior of their students' companions; for they did not. Maybe estimates of friends' misbehavior make more reliable distinctions because, at our initial interviews with them, perhaps before they had learned to trust us with their confessions, the reports of their friends' misbehavior were the more accurate gauge of their own. In any case, buoyant students' attitudes toward school are reliably related to their own behavior even after taking into account their friends' behavior. It seems reasonable to conclude that the effect of the alternative schools was not mediated or conditioned by the degree of misbehavior of their students' friends.

Students' Relationships with Their Parents

Many educators have despaired of doing anything about their troublesome students because the students' parents, they say, are responsible in the senses both of being the cause of the problem and having the obligation to solve it. But these parents are typically uncooperative. So, since the schools cannot change the parents, the schools are powerless. But, as Bowman's alternative school, Persons's group therapy, and Massimo and Shore's social case work studies have shown, programs can be effective without directly involving youths' parents. Undoubtedly parents are a factor in delinquency: the parental relationships of heavily delinquent youth have consistently been found to be worse than those of the less delinquent. But obviously this does not necessarily mean that parental relationships are the only factor and that youngsters will become better behaved only if these relationships improve.

We explored the influence exerted by our participants' relationships with their parents in order to discover whether it was crucial to the change process. We focused on the affectional relationships between parents and adolescent as the adolescent perceived them. We chose this focus because previous studies had shown that affection was more important than other relational properties, like the autonomy the adolescent was given, and it seemed to reflect best the effective elements of the relationship. We measured the affection that the adolescents felt between themselves and their parents with a card-sorting technique we had found in our national studies to be related to delinquent behavior. Respondents were given a set of cards to sort into four piles, thus indicating how true the statement on each card was of their relationship with their father or mother. For example, the statements included, "I feel close to my father" and "my mother gives me the right amount of affection." We generated two scores for each respondent, one for the paternal and one for the maternal relationship.

The correlations between these measures of parent/adolescent affection and respondents' reports of their delinquent behavior at waves 1 and 3, while in the expected negative direction, are unexpectedly low and in a few cases, positive. They range from .21 (p = .15) to $-.32$ ($p = .01$) and only the last, between beset students' delinquent behavior and their relationship with their mothers, is reliably different from zero. It seems then that our respondents' relationships with their parents are not as closely associated with their misbehavior as is generally the case among American teenagers. One reason may be that the youth in this study were almost all highly delinquent, well into the upper range of the general population. Differences in delinquency among youth at that high level may simply not be much further affected by differences in their relationships with their parents.

There is another respect in which the association between parental relations and delinquency differs for these students compared to our national samples. Previous studies have shown that the relationship with the father weighs more heavily in the delinquency equation than the relationship with the mother. Among these students however, the relationship with the mother seems more important. When we entered scores for both parental relationships in a series of regression equations as joint predictors to delinquent or disruptive behavior, the partial correlations of the mother's relationship were higher and more consistently negative. One implication of this is that if the schools were to somehow affect students through the students' relationships with their parents, the maternal relationships were more crucial.

Actually the alternative programs had little effect on their students' relationships with their mothers (see figs. 26 and 27). The reader may remember that the parental relationships of the conventional and alternative students did not differ at the outset. Similarly, there were few differences at the close of this study. The amount of affection reported between mothers and their adolescents at wave 3, adjusted for baseline differences, was unreliably less affectionate among the alternative students. But the alternative students reported a reliably better relationship with their fathers ($p = .05$) (see figs. 28 and 29). The buoyant students were wholly responsible for this latter difference ($p = .02$); the difference among beset students was in the same direction but negligible ($p = .91$).

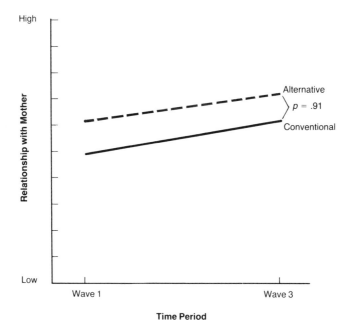

Fig. 26. Change in relationship with mother for *buoyant* alternative ($n = 41$) and conventional ($n = 47$) school students

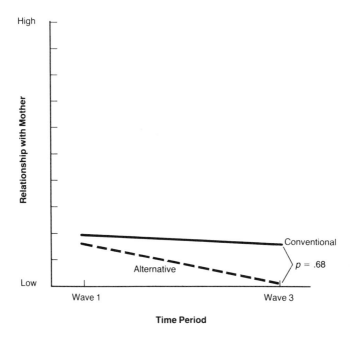

Fig. 27. Change in relationship with mother for *beset* alternative ($n = 27$) and conventional ($n = 20$) school students

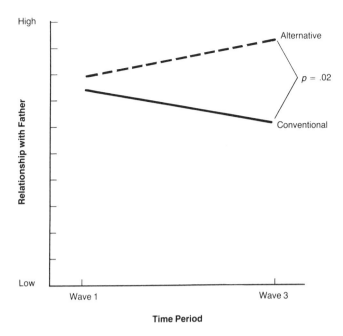

Fig. 28. Change in relationship with father for *buoyant* alternative ($n = 31$) and conventional ($n = 35$) school students

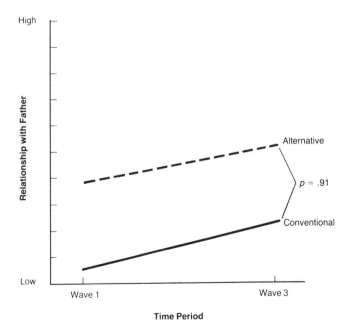

Fig. 29. Change in relationship with father for *beset* alternative ($n = 21$) and conventional ($n = 19$) school students

There is some evidence that the greater effectiveness of the Alpha program was due to improvements in its students' relationships with their parents. The most reliable ($p = .02$) difference in alternative and conventional students' parental relationships was found in the relationship to fathers of Alpha's buoyant students, those on whom Alpha had its markedly positive effects. The parental relationships of Alpha's beset students on the other hand were marginally worse than the conventional students ($p = .10$). Buoyant students' paternal relationships fared better over the course of the study at Beta and ACE too, compared to the respective conventional comparison groups, but not as much better as at Alpha.

But while the alternative schools, especially Alpha, may have indirectly exerted some positive influence on their buoyant students' relationships with their fathers, that influence did not appear to affect buoyant students' behavior much, independent of the students' attitudes toward school. As table 19 shows, buoyant students' attitudes toward school were more negatively related to their misbehavior than their relationship with either their fathers or their mothers. But in contrast, the beset students' relationships with their mothers were more negatively related to their misbehavior than their attitudes toward school were. Furthermore, at the outset of the study, buoyant students' relationships with their fathers and their mothers were more closely related to their misbehavior than they were a year later; but these correlations grew more negative in the same time period among the beset students. The picture presented by the data in table 19 indicates that the behavior of the buoyant students is more closely related to how they feel about school. This is not true of the beset students, among whom neither attitudes toward school nor relationships with parents seem important, except perhaps for their relationships with their mothers.

These data suggest that experiences at school can make a difference in the behavior of buoyant students, independent of the students' relationships with their parents. At no place in our analyses of our data did we find that the effects of the social psychological processes going on in the various schools were conditioned by or superseded by buoyant students' parental relationships. While increasing affection between parents and adolescents probably will improve adolescents' behavior, it is not a necessary condition.

Self-Esteem
Our theory of a particular kind of alternative school as a means for reducing disruptive and delinquent behavior identifies

TABLE 19. Attitudes toward School and Relationships with Parents as Joint Predictors of Disruptive and Delinquent Behaviors among Buoyant and Beset Students at Waves 1 and 3

	Disruptive Behavior										Delinquent Behavior									
	Attitude toward School			Relationship with Father		Attitude toward School			Relationship with Mother		Attitude toward School			Relationship with Father		Attitude toward School			Relationship with Mother	
	n	r	p	r	p	n	r	p	r	p	n	r	p	r	p	n	r	p	r	p
Wave 1																				
Buoyant	64	−.47	<.01	−.11	.37	81	−.31	.004	−.24	.03	64	−.45	<.01	−.23	.07	81	−.38	<.001	−.21	.06
Beset	35	.04	.82	.09	.61	43	.23	.14	−.07	.68	35	−.07	.71	.01	.97	43	.17	.27	−.20	.21
Wave 3																				
Buoyant	56	−.54	<.01	−.00	.97	69	−.41	<.001	.01	.96	54	−.31	.02	.10	.45	69	−.25	.04	−.05	.66
Beset	32	−.29	.11	−.05	.76	37	−.15	.38	−.23	.19	32	−.17	.36	−.11	.57	37	−.10	.56	−.38	.02

Note: Entries are partial correlations of attitudes toward school and relationships with fathers or mothers with each kind of misbehavior. The correlations were generated by multiple regression equations.

youngsters' self-esteem as a key variable. In this respect, the theory is part of a broader theory about the nature and causes of delinquent behavior. The theory posits that delinquency is in defense of a derogated self-image, that delinquency is provoked by low self-esteem. In earlier research we had demonstrated that older adolescent boys whose conscious self-esteem was above average but whose unconscious self-esteem was below average were markedly more delinquent than others with different patterns of conscious and unconscious self-esteem. We hypothesized therefore that the alternative school experience, with its greater proportion of scholastic success and supportive teachers, would be effective insofar as it improved students' unconscious self-esteem.

In order to test this hypothesis, we measured unconscious self-esteem with the projective test of the Social Self-Construct described earlier, and we employed two measures of conscious self-esteem, also described earlier.

We found that the alternative schools had no significant effect on the self-esteem of their students. There were some marked shifts in the self-esteem of most of the students during the course of the study: as measured by Bachman's revision of Rosenberg's measure, the conscious self-esteem of the buoyant students and the beset alternative students declined ($p < .05$); the conscious self-esteem of the beset conventional students was unreliably higher (see figs. 30 and 31). There were no reliable trends on either of the other two measures (see figs. 32 and 33). We have seen that the behavior and performance in school of the buoyant alternative students improved during this period, but this apparently occurred without marked change in their unconscious self-esteem and in the face of a decline in their conscious self-esteem, at least as reflected by one measure. Self-esteem was not so crucial to the social psychological process of change as we had expected it to be. Changes in academic prospects, commitment to the role of student, and attitudes toward school made a difference for the buoyant alternative students in the absence of differential change in their self-esteem.

The data in table 20 bring out the relative importance of self-esteem in the change process. The figures were generated by a set of regression equations in which the three measures of self-esteem were each entered with the measure of attitude toward school to predict scores for disruptive and delinquent behavior at wave 3 that were adjusted for baseline levels at wave 1. Scores on attitudes toward school were chosen to represent the school-related variables because, as we have noted, they seem to summarize the effects of the school experience best. Not all the school-related variables or the

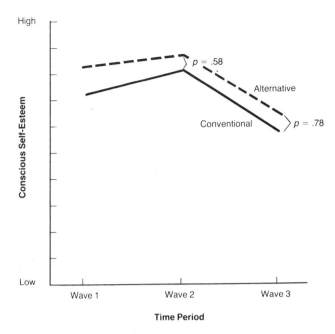

Fig. 30. Changes in conscious self-esteem for *buoyant* alternative ($n = 44$) and conventional ($n = 39$) school students

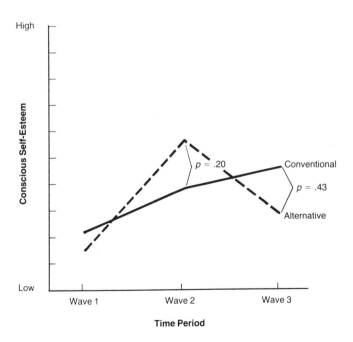

Fig. 31. Changes in conscious self-esteem for *beset* alternative ($n = 21$) and conventional ($n = 18$) school students

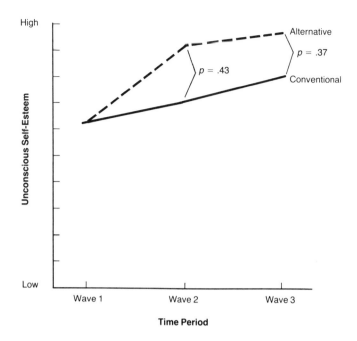

Fig. 32. Changes in unconscious self-esteem for *buoyant* alternative ($n = 38$) and conventional ($n = 36$) school students

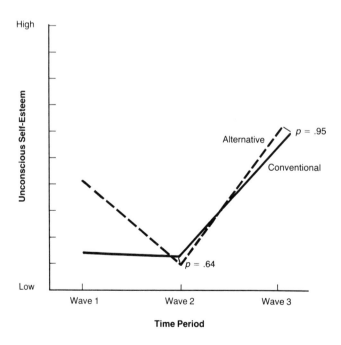

Fig. 33. Changes in unconscious self-esteem for *beset* alternative ($n = 20$) and conventional ($n = 18$) school students

TABLE 20. Attitudes toward School and Self-Esteem as Joint Predictors of Disruptive and Delinquent Behaviors among Buoyant and Beset Students at Wave 3

	Attitudes toward School			Self-Esteem (Rosenberg/Bachman)		Attitudes toward School			Self-Esteem (Semantic Differential)		Attitudes toward School			Self-Esteem (Self-social Construct)	
	n	r	p	r	p	n	r	p	r	p	n	r	p	r	p
Disruptive Behavior															
Buoyant	75	−.38	<.001	−.07	.54	74	−.39	<.001	−.07	.58	71	−.43	<.001	−.21	.08
Beset	42	.13	.41	−.40	.01	42	.19	.24	−.32	.04	41	.02	.92	.11	.52
Delinquent Behavior															
Buoyant	93	−.19	.07	−.03	.78	92	−.19	.07	−.06	.57	89	−.17	.12	−.04	.72
Beset	49	.08	.60	−.37	.01	49	.18	.22	−.41	.004	48	.00	1.0	.00	.99

three measures of self-esteem could be entered in the same regression equation because that would have burdened the number of cases in the equations with too many predictors and yield unstable results. So the scores of attitudes toward school were entered to predict jointly with each of the measures of self-esteem in separate equations. The figures presented in table 20 are the resulting partial correlations of the two predictors with disruptive and delinquent behavior respectively. The informative features in these data are the comparisons between the partial correlations of attitudes toward school and each measure of self-esteem, and how those comparisons differ among the buoyant and the beset students. Buoyant students' attitudes toward school consistently predict better to both disruptive and delinquent behaviors; beset students' self-esteem predicts better in every case but one. Furthermore, conscious self-esteem is in no case a reliable predictor of the buoyant students' behavior; but it is a reliable predictor of the beset students'. Unconscious self-esteem may have been related to buoyant students' disruptive behavior in school, but it was probably not related to their delinquent behavior in the community.

These data support the generalization that attitudes toward school and the other components of the model of change are more determinative of the behavior of buoyant than of beset youth. More important for the latter are conscious self-esteem or factors related to self-esteem but probably unrelated to scholastic experiences. This generalization is consistent with and helps us to understand why the alternative schools were more effective in reducing the disruptive and delinquent behavior of their buoyant students. Since the schools did not improve the self-esteem of any of its students, they were not able, through that dynamic, to help their beset students.

Chapter 6

Conclusions

The assertion that poor scholastic experiences are significant causes of delinquent and disruptive behavior, particularly at school, received strong support in this study. The importance of two specific components of scholastic experiences, scholastic performance as reflected by grades and relationships with teachers, are underlined by the findings. We found that the perception of flexibility of their scholastic program is pivotal to the students' beliefs that they can succeed as students and that their teachers will give them the social support that they need. These beliefs in turn encourage a more positive attitude toward schools and schooling generally. When students in an alternative program develop more confidence in themselves as students, more commitment to their education, and better global attitudes toward school, improvement in their behavior and performance persist for most of them even when they reenter a conventional program which they do not regard as so flexible.

But we found that this process did not work so well with beset students, who entered the alternative schools unusually anxious and depressed. We believe that this finding may be significant for our general understanding of delinquency, specifically for the identification of types of delinquents.

Types of Delinquents

Students of delinquency have searched for a useful typology of delinquents for at least three reasons. One is the observation that heavily delinquent youth are apparently so different from one another that it has seemed inconceivable that they are all cut from the same cloth. Another reason is the frustration over the frequent failures of delinquency treatment programs. Since virtually every program seems to be successful with some of their clients even while they do not affect most of them, it seems reasonable to suppose that there are types of delinquents who are responsive to some interventions and not others. Finally, no one theory of delinquency has been able to explain the behavior of all delinquents. In every study there are many exceptions even when the overall results support the theoretical hypotheses.

There have been many essays at identifying types of delinquents. Some typologies are based on the kinds of offenses youth have committed, others on responses to personality tests (Ferdinand 1966; Gold and Petronio 1980). The typology that seems to have stood up best to empirical test is Hewitt and Jenkins' (1947) distinction between socialized and unsocialized delinquents. The differentiation of buoyant from beset students in our findings supports this typology. One major distinction between the two types is that the socialized delinquents are integrated into peer groups, albeit predominantly delinquent ones, while the unsocialized delinquents are not. We wish in retrospect that we had asked students whether their disruptive and delinquent behaviors in school and out were in concert with peers or alone. We suspect that the beset students are mainly loners. We have pointed out that, compared to the buoyant students, the beset feel more often that they cannot count on their friends.

In order to qualify as types, the socialized/buoyant and the unsocialized/beset would have to differ sharply enough from one another in enough ways so that the differences are qualitative. Simply being more or less anxious and depressed is not sufficient to establish types. That we have found the two categories to be different in some other ways as well is a beginning toward justifying the typology. We feel it would be worthwhile both theoretically and practically to pursue this further, trying to establish with more objective measures what Hewitt and Jenkins proposed on the basis of clinical evidence and insight.

Meanwhile, the question arises of whether school-based programs might better screen out manifestly depressed and anxious students because the programs are less likely to help them. Such screening would be advisable if anxiety and depression could be diagnosed accurately. But this is difficult under the best of circumstances and few school systems have the resources to do this well. It seems wiser to us, therefore, to employ alternative school programs in the diagnostic process: if certain students' behavior does not improve despite their greater satisfaction with the alternative program, then a search for other points of intervention might be made. It may be wise meanwhile to permit beset students to remain in alternative schools for a longer period, perhaps even to graduate from them, because they seem to feel better while they are there.

Self-Esteem

We had hypothesized that improvement in students' self-esteem, particularly at the unconscious level, would be a key mediator between alternative programs and changes in students' behavior. The data do not support this hypothesis. We found little change in unconscious levels of students' self-esteem and a general decline in students' conscious self-esteem over the course of our observations. Nevertheless, the alternative programs achieved significant positive changes among their buoyant students.

There are several plausible interpretations of our findings about self-esteem. One is that youngsters' disruptive and delinquent behavior is not so much provoked by their need to defend against threats to their self-image as it is controlled by their commitments to conventional social institutions. We note that the effectiveness of the alternative programs was mediated by students' growing optimism about their chances to succeed at school and by their greater commitment to the role of student. They may be said to have acquired a new stake in schooling; and having thus something to lose if they were expelled, had something to gain by behaving better and trying harder. This interpretation is in close accord with Hirschi's (1969) theory of social control which asserts that no special provocation, such as a derogated self-image, is necessary to explain why youngsters become disruptive and delinquent in the absence of social control. But we have cited data from other studies which suggest that a derogated self-image is a characteristic of heavily delinquent youth, so a hypothesis about the provocative nature of low self-esteem should not be dismissed too early.

We also note that the positive effects of the alternative schools were narrow, being most clearly on students' behavior at school and not reliably on delinquent behavior in the community. Perhaps the effects were narrow because the mediating changes were limited to school-related optimism and commitment. It is possible that unless or until youngsters' scholastic experiences enhance self-esteem globally, they will not have a global effect on their misbehavior. We have assumed that performance at school is highly salient to adolescents in western culture, and that being good at it would enhance self-esteem globally. Perhaps we have overestimated the breadth of its impact.

On the other hand, it may be that the timing of our final interview with the students, one term after they had returned to the conventional schools, did not allow sufficiently for youngsters' self-esteem to change. The students may not yet have been altogether convinced of their ability to make it through school, despite their greater optimism. If this is the case, then we would expect that a follow-up study of these students will demonstrate the importance of self-esteem as a mediator for a wider and enduring change in their behavior.

There is one ominous sign in our data on self-esteem; the conscious self-esteem of the buoyant students and of the beset alternative students had declined significantly from our first to our third interviews with them. If it is true that low conscious self-esteem is provocative to disruptive and delinquent behavior, as Kaplan has found (1980), then we can expect a resurgence of misbehavior in the future. Or, if for some reason delinquency proves to be an inadequate defense, then we can expect increased anxiety and depression. A follow-up study would check these expectations.

Families and Friends

Our findings relating to students' families and friends also have theoretical and practical implications. Change in the buoyant students' behavior and scholastic performance, we found, did not depend upon improved relationships with their parents or diminished delinquency among their friends. These data speak to the salience of scholastic experiences, which seem to have marked influence in their own right, whether as sources of provocation or of social control. It is likely that the salience of schooling is pervasive throughout western culture, but it is plausible that there are subcultural differences. School-based programs may not be so effective in some subcultures, independent of other influences like families and friends. For example, we are mindful that almost all the students in our study were white suburbanites. Would alternative programs like the ones we observed work among black residents of the inner city? We think so, but of course, they would have to be tried. We think so because there are sufficient data in hand to indicate that schooling is certainly no less salient for black adolescents and their parents and perhaps even more salient (Bachman 1970; Coleman et al. 1966; Schab 1968).

We are not surprised that the alternative schools had independent positive effects on the behavior of buoyant students, at least at school. After all, the thrust of adolescence in our culture is to become more autonomous from parents and more serious about schoolwork. While most adolescents are still closely bound in many ways to their parents, the familial ties of most heavily delinquent youngsters are weaker. Our data reflect this: the students' attitudes toward school were more closely related to their delinquency than were their relationships with their parents. A possible exception to this generalization is the beset students' relationships with their mothers, which seemed more closely related to their behavior. This is consistent with our observation that the alternative programs were not effective with beset students because school was not the main source of their problems.

At the same time that adolescents are becoming more independent of parental influence, they are becoming more involved with their friends and peers. One might expect therefore that the delinquent tendencies of students' friends would be important influences on the students' behavior. But, as we have said, having delinquent friends is more likely a consequence of needing support for one's own delinquent behavior than a cause of that behavior. Buoyant students' disruptive and delinquent behavior at school declined even while they were reporting no change in their friends' behavior. We expect that students whose improved performance and behavior persist will however eventually begin to select less delinquent friends.

The practical significance of our findings relating to students' parents and friends is that educators need not depend upon reaching disruptive students' parents or changing disruptive students' friendship patterns in order to reduce disruption in their schools. Alternative programs of the kind we have observed can be independently effective with their more buoyant students. But it may be important that someone intervene with the parents of the beset students who do not respond positively to an alternative school.

Flexibility

Of particular practical significance is our finding that students' perceptions of their alternative school being flexible is critical to positive change. Many of the concrete options for designing alternative programs may be selected on the basis of the general principle of enhancing flexibility. Flexibility in this instance means taking into account the individual students' needs, fears, abilities, and mood in conducting the daily business of education. We regard *flexibility* as another term for personal-ity or the absence of rigid role regulation of social interactions. It is manifested in part by a relative suspension of the conventional rules governing how teachers and students behave toward one another. Another manifestation is the alteration of planned activities to accommodate to the mood of the class as a whole.

For example, one option for an alternative program is to house it in a building separate from the conventional high school that the students would ordinarily attend. Our observation of the schools in this study suggest to us that being in separate buildings contributed a great deal to the flexibility of the programs. The more casual comings and goings of alternative students, the occasionally higher noise level, the regular availability of coffee and a place to smoke, and other deliberate informalities that created the ambience of the alternative programs probably could not have been tolerated in the midst of a conventional comprehensive secondary school. At the same time, the potential danger of stigmatization by the implication of isolation and quarantine did not materialize, according to our data. The proximity of the separate facilities to the conventional junior and senior high schools was useful because it facilitated the attendance of students in selected classes and students' transitions back to the conventional schools.

For another example: There seems to be a growing consensus among educators, despite the lack of any reliable data, that the principal is a major determinant of the level of disruptiveness in a school. Furthermore, the consensus seems to be that firm discipline and organization are the hallmarks of the effective principal. Our data on the importance of perceived flexibility suggest, on the other hand, that disruptive students may not respond so well to the projection of such a principal's style onto the school program if discipline and organization mean inflexibility. Certain students may be disruptive because they have chronic problems dealing with authority and because their frequent experiences of failure in school make any universal standards of behavior and performance threatening to them. If the principal is indeed a key element in minimizing school disruption, this study suggests that it is because his or her administration permits and encourages the staff to develop more personal relationships even with the most disruptive students and to accommodate to their individuality.

A recent report by Gary D. Gottfredson and his colleagues (1981) underscores the importance of flexibility in school administration. These researchers investigated the characteristics of schools that determined the frequency and seriousness with which teachers and students were robbed, assaulted, or threatened by students. They employed the data collected in NIE's Safe School Study

(1978) from a national sample of 642 public secondary schools. The teachers and students reported their experiences of being victimized in response to anonymous questionnaires. The authors conclude that:

> The soundness of a school's administration—indexed by measures of teacher-administration cooperation, ratings of the principal's behavior, *the perceived fairness and clarity of the school rules, and student influence on the way the school is run and their attachment to the school*—is linked to teacher reports of victimization in both junior and senior high schools. . . . Furthermore, the soundness of school administration is linked with all measures of student victimization in both junior and senior high schools, except for the reports of girls in senior high schools of robberies and attacks which are relatively unpredictable by any school or community characteristic. The models always imply that the better the administration the less the victimization. (P. 89, italics added)

Our findings reveal a process by which the flexibility of school administration leads to attachment to the school and thence a decline in disruptive behavior. Our findings also suggest that flexibility is critical because it affects certain of the potentially most disruptive students. We are inclined to infer from our findings that the essential aspects of flexibility are *not* manifested primarily in institutional arrangements such as a fair student code and a democratic and responsive student government. Important as these may be to the education of American adolescents, they may not be critical to the level of disruption in a school. Rather, we believe, the capacity of the school's administration to bend the rules and arrangements to the needs of the most ill-suited students may lie at the core of effective flexibility. It seems plausible that the other more generalized institutionalized manifestations of flexibility are related to this capacity. This line of thought suggests that safer conventional schools are those whose administration more nearly resembles the management of the kind of alternative school that we studied. But, of course, these alternative schools, designed especially for the education and socialization of the most disruptive students, are flexible in this sense to a much greater extreme.

We recognize that the desirable flexibility of alternative schools contains an element of unfairness. This unfairness, we think, is a major source of opposition to alternative schools among faculty and staff of conventional schools. Conventional school teachers quite rightly feel strongly their obligation to treat their students evenhandedly, which includes holding them equally to scholastic standards. But it is apparent that this principle is not followed in the kind of alternative school we observed in this study. So these alternative schools are open to the charge that their students earn scholastic credits with less effort, that they receive passing grades for less than passable work, and that they are privileged to break ordinary school rules. And this, it is pointed out, as a consequence of behaving intolerably badly! But we need to remember that the intolerable behavior was generated under conditions of fixed standards for performance and behavior, applied evenhandedly. These are conditions with which for whatever reasons, disruptive students are developmentally unable to deal. It is arguable, nevertheless, that adolescents need to learn to deal with these conditions, for their school is a reflection of the society the schools serve. And it is also arguable that, according to our data, suspension of these conditions is efficacious for that learning to occur, at least by students who are not extremely anxious and depressed. Tailoring the level and pace of learning to the individual student's abilities and interests, and fostering personal relations between teachers and students contradict our conventional sense of fairness. Psychologically, however, the conditions of the alternative schools seemed to their students more fair than the conventional schools'.

The tension between the values of flexibility and fairness in alternative schooling is related to another, broader contemporary debate in the field of delinquency treatment and prevention, indeed in the whole field of intervention to resolve social problems. The debate has typically been posed as "system blame" versus "victim blame." Who or what is "responsible" for delinquent, disruptive behavior at school, and who or what should change in order to ameliorate the problem? On the one side are those who indict social conditions—and cast heavily delinquent youth as victims. They point to the schools, the economy, the supposed breakdown of family life, an evil *Zeitgeist*, etc., as the causes of delinquency, and they insist that these must be changed. Some alternative educators are in this camp. They believe that conventional education is at fault, not only for provoking some youth to disruptive and delinquent behavior but also for its treatment of students generally. They want the kinds of alternative schools included in this study to be models for education and see themselves at the forefront of a movement to accomplish this. Among their guiding texts are Postman and Weingartner's

Teaching as a Subversive Activity (1969) and Kozol's indictment of American public education, *The Night Is Dark and I Am Far from Home* (1980). They frequently get along badly with their colleagues at the conventional schools.

On the other side are those who believe that heavily delinquent, disruptive students are responsible for their own behavior. These people have witnessed incidents of truancy, vandalism, even of personal violence, and they can identify the chronic troublemakers. They know that the overwhelming majority of students at their schools—living in the same neighborhoods, many with apparently as poor homes—do not do such things. They find such behavior intolerable because it threatens to make the school impossible and it violates basic morality. They believe that the schools are worth preserving as they are because they will benefit most students and the society of which the schools are an integral part. Some will say frankly that they do not care whether the small number of troublemakers get an education at all, so long as these kids are removed from the schools they disrupt. If these students want the privilege of an education—and it often appears that they do not, anyway—then they must change in order to merit it.

Our own view is that this debate is spurious. We do not think that we have set up straw men here, either. In the course of conducting this study and talking about it to many audiences, we have heard both sides of the argument stated pretty much as we have summarized them. Our argument derives from our social psychological perspective. Certainly the attitude, motives, and abilities of the youngsters are responsible in a real sense for their behavior, and therefore their behavior will not change much without psychological change. But the youngsters' social environment is largely responsible for their attitudes, motives, and abilities, and therefore, if these are to change, the relevant environment must change. Our hypothesis, which this study has confirmed for the majority of the students, has been that the school is a significant part of the socializing environment. If that "system" changes in appropriate ways, it will generate positive change among the youngsters. The "victim" and the "system" encounter one another, each with its particular characteristics, and the effect of each on the other comes from their encounter. The school system has certain alternatives available to it to effectively change the conditions of its encounters with disruptive students by changing itself. It can thereby so affect the students that students and institutions can encounter one another in ways more favorable to both.

It is hard to say who is "responsible" for the beset students, or who should be. We have suggested that the conditions that provoke them to disruptive behavior may not be located in their schools. On the other hand, the environment of their schools seems to have a substantial effect on their behavior; after all, the beset students did not disrupt their alternative schools even if the effect did not persist when they returned to conventional schools. In any case, it is likely that changing the school system alone will not suffice to improve the quality of its future encounters with beset students. Other parts of the students' environments will probably have to change. Wherever that is—their homes are implicated—is where the "responsibility" lies. But other agencies may need to act in order to solve the problem.

Research Strategy

We close with some reflection on the research process that produced the findings we have been discussing.

We feel that this study confirms the value of field research that is simultaneously theoretical and evaluative. We believe that this study has to some degree advanced our understanding of education, of delinquency, and of adolescence; and that it has also demonstrated the practical worth of a particular intervention in a serious social problem. We want at this point to consider what features of this study were important for making whatever contribution it has made. These features fall roughly into two categories: What should be studied? And how should the research be designed?

We feel that it is extremely important to study the underlying process by which programs seek to achieve their goals rather than focusing solely on outcomes. Whether programs are successful will vary from student to student, teacher to teacher, program to program. Consider the present study. Simple assessment of the outcomes of the three programs would have come to the conclusion that they were only marginally effective in reducing the disruptive behavior of their students in school in comparison to the conventional students. (Note that if there had been no comparison groups, the three programs would have appeared quite successful.) But exploration of the underlying processes has shown that those programs did indeed produce marked change in particular attitudes and perceptions of certain identifiable students in a way conducive to better behavior and greater scholastic achievement. A summative evaluation that considered merely the outcome could not have produced these findings.

Conceptual frameworks or theoretical models are invaluable for the identification of underlying processes. We might have focused this research on many different processes. We claim no special prescience in having chosen to study some processes that proved to make a significant difference. We were guided by the experience of educators and researchers who have considered this problem before and who have in various degrees articulated their experiences in theoretical terms. With a theory, it is possible to recognize different practices as instances of the same process. The three alternative programs we studied were in many ways quite different from one another. Some of those differences made a difference in the way their students responded to them, yet despite their apparent differences, the programs also had much in common. Our theory led us to focus on those common elements and to observe the processes which were set in motion as a result. Conceptualizing underlying processes also makes possible the dissemination of successful program elements without having to rely on exact replications of a particular set of conditions, staff, and resources. That is because conceptually guided evaluations not only tell which programs work, but also identify the essential features and tell for whom, under what circumstances, and why the program is likely to work.

Had we ignored the possibility that the alternative schools had recruited different types of students, some of whom would not respond favorably to their programs, we might have missed the significant effects that the programs had on the buoyant students' behavior and performance. It was not just luck or a stroke of serendipity that we had measured the students' anxiety and depression and tested whether they conditioned students' responses to the programs. The problem of types of delinquents has vexed scholars for some time, and theories have been developed about it. We took some of this theorizing as a guide to our research, and it proved very useful.

Theoretically guided investigation of the processes of social intervention will be needed in order to find ways of helping the beset students and their schools. In general, in order to decide what to do about less than satisfactory results, one needs to know why they occurred. They could happen for several reasons. A program may be quite effective in its implementation of prescribed methods and processes, but these methods may be irrelevant to the desired outcomes. The methods and processes might be altogether appropriate, but the program falls short of implementing them. Or, the program might implement the appropriate methods for its goals, but for the wrong students. In the present case, the alternative schools apparently did invoke effective processes; and even the beset students felt their impact. But they were insufficient to maintain the desired change when the beset students returned to their conventional schools. The puzzle of the beset students has been clarified a little. We need now to theorize more about what in the students and in their environment is responsible for their unfavorable encounters and test the hypotheses that emerge.

The matter of research designs is more controversial. Some hold that only through randomized designs built into the programs can evaluation research provide valid and useful information. Yet, as we discovered, random selection of students is hard to arrange, even with a well-defined and appropriate pool of eligible recipients in the context of a mutually agreed-upon research design. When it is possible to implement random assignment, field research should by all means take advantage of the opportunity. The certainty of the study's conclusions will be significantly improved.

We were however unable to implement our planned randomized research design. Does this vitiate this study under the doctrine that unless the design is a randomized one, the outcomes cannot be trusted? A corollary to the doctrine is that unless random-design research can be done, none should be done. We are in agreement with the desirability of randomized designs. We also are in agreement with the principle that intervention programs should be assessed and evaluated. When the first principle precludes the second, we feel that carefully conducted quasi-experimental or other suitable methods of research and evaluation are to be preferred to none at all (Cook and Campbell 1976). We are confident of the validity of the findings we have presented in this report. Whatever contribution they represent would not have been made had we insisted either on randomized assignment or no research at all.

Of course, the nonrandom assignment of students is not the only source of uncertainty in our findings. We have dealt in statistical probabilities at conventionally respectable levels of likelihood; we have studied programs operating under a rather narrow set of cultural conditions; and the effects we have observed have been only short-term; among other things. It has become virtually a ritual incantation to conclude research reports such as this with a call "for further research." We will not exempt ourselves from the ritual. In truth, there is compelling theoretical and practical need to continue the systematic study of a promising social innovation.

Bibliography

Anderson, B. D. 1973. "School Bureaucratization and Alienation from High School." *Sociology of Education* 46:315–34.

Arnove, R. 1978. *Alternative Schools for Disruptive Youth.* Bloomington: Indiana University School of Education.

Aronson, E., and Mettee, D. R. 1968. "Dishonest Behavior as a Function of Differential Levels of Induced Self-esteem." *Journal of Personality and Social Psychology* 9:121–27.

Bachman, J. G. 1970. *Youth in Transition: Volume II. The Impact of Family Background and Intelligence on Tenth Grade Boys.* Ann Arbor: Institute for Social Research.

———. 1972. *Young Men in High School and Beyond: A Summary of Findings from the Youth in Transition Project.* Final report to the U.S. Department of Health, Education, and Welfare.

Bachman, J. G.; Kahn, R. L.; Mednick, M. T.; Davidson, T.; and Johnston, L. 1967. *Youth in Transition: Volume I. Blueprint for a Longitudinal Study of Adolescent Boys.* Ann Arbor: Institute for Social Research.

Bachman, J. G.; O'Malley, P. M.; and Johnston, J. 1978. *Adolescence to Adulthood—Stability and Change in the Lives of Young Men.* Ann Arbor: Institute for Social Research.

Bennett, V. D. C. N.d. An Investigation of the Relationships among Children's Self-Concept, Achievement, Intelligence, Body Size, and the Size of Their Figure Drawing. Mimeographed.

Berger, M. 1974. *Violence in the Schools: Causes and Remedies.* Bloomington, Ind.: Phi Delta Kappa Educational Foundation.

Berman, S. M. 1976. "Validation of Social Self-esteem as an Experimental Index of Delinquent Behavior." *Perceptual and Motor Skills* 43:848–50.

Bledsoe, J. C. 1964. "Self-concepts of Children and Their Intelligence, Achievement, Interests and Anxiety." *Journal of Individual Psychology* 20:55–58.

Bowman, P. H. 1959. "Effects of a Revised School Program on Potential Delinquents." *Annals of the American Academy of Political and Social Science* 322:53–62.

Cattell, R. B., and Warburton, F. W. 1967. *Objective Personality and Motivation Tests.* Urbana: University of Illinois Press.

Cobb, S.; Brooks, G. H.; Kasl, S. V.; and Connelly, W. E. 1966. "The Health of People Changing Jobs: A Description of a Longitudinal Study." *American Journal of Public Health* 56:1476–81.

Cohen, A. K. 1955. *Delinquent Boys.* Glencoe: The Free Press.

Coleman, J. S. 1961. *The Adolescent Society.* New York: The Free Press of Glencoe.

Coleman, J. S.; Campbell, E. Q.; Hobson, C. J.; McPartland, J.; Mood, A. M.; Weinfeld, F. D.; and York, R. L. 1966. *Equality of Educational Opportunity.* Washington, D.C.: U.S. Government Printing Office.

Cook, T. D., and Campbell, D. T. 1976. "The Design and Conduct of Quasi Experiments and True Experiments in Field Settings." In *Handbook of Industrial and Organizational Psychology,* edited by M. D. Dunnette. Chicago: Rand McNally.

Davies, J. G. V., and Maliphant, R. 1971. "Autonomic Responses of Male Adolescents Exhibiting Refractory Behavior in School." *Journal of Child Psychology and Psychiatry* 12:115–27.

Dawes, R. 1979. "The Robust Beauty of Improper Linear Models." *American Psychologist* 34:571–83.

Deal, T. E., and Nolan, R. R. 1978. *Alternative Schools.* Chicago: Nelson-Hall.

Douvan, E., and Adelson, J. 1966. *The Adolescent Experience.* New York: Wiley.

Dudek, S. Z., and Lester, E. P. N.d. "The Good Child Facade in Chronic Underachievers." Montreal: Department of Psychiatry, McGill University. Mimeographed.

Duke, D. L. 1978. *The Retransformation of the School.* Chicago: Nelson-Hall.

Elliott, D. S. 1966. "Delinquency, School Attendance and Dropout." *Social Problems* 13:307–14.

Elliott, D. S., and Voss, H. L. 1974. *Delinquency and Dropout.* Lexington, Mass.: D. C. Heath.

Epps, E. G. 1969. *Family and Achievement: A Study of the Relations of Family Background to Achievement Orientation and Performance among Urban Negro High School Students.* Ann Arbor: Institute for Social Research.

Epstein, J. L., and McPartland, J. M. 1976a. "The Concept and Measurement of the Quality of School Life." *American Educational Research Journal* 13:115–30.

———. 1976b. *Summary of Manual for the Quality of School Life Scale.* Baltimore: Johns Hopkins University Center for the Social Organization of Schools.

Erikson, E. 1968. *Identity: Youth and Crisis.* New York: Norton.

Farrington, D. P. 1979. "Longitudinal Research on Crime and Delinquency." In *Crime and Justice 1978: An Annual Review of Criminal Justice Research,* edited by N. Morris and M. Tonty. Chicago: University of Chicago Press.

Farrington, D. P., and West, D. J. 1979. "The Cambridge Study in Delinquent Development." In *An Empirical Basis for Primary Prevention:*

Prospective Longitudinal Research in Europe, edited by S. A. Mednick and A. E. Baert. New York: Oxford University Press.

Feldhusen, J. F.; Denny, T.; and Condon, C. F. 1965. "Anxiety, Divergent Thinking, and Achievement." *Journal of Educational Psychology* 56:40–45.

Feldhusen, J. F.; Thurston, J. R.; and Benning, J. J. 1971. "Prediction Academic Achievement of Children who Display Aggressive-Disruptive Classroom Behavior." Paper presented at the annual meeting of the American Educational Research Association, New York City.

Ferdinand, T. N. 1966. *Typologies of Delinquency.* New York: Random House.

Flanders, N. A. 1965. *Teacher Influence, Pupil Attitudes and Achievement.* Washington, D.C.: U.S. Department of Health, Education, and Welfare.

———. 1970. *Analyzing Teaching Behavior.* Reading, Mass.: Addison-Wesley.

Fox, D. J., and Guire, K. E. 1976. *Documentation for MIDAS.* 3d ed. Ann Arbor: Statistical Research Laboratory, The University of Michigan.

Glasser, W. 1969. *Schools Without Failure.* New York: Harper and Row.

Glueck, S., and Glueck, E. 1950. *Unraveling Juvenile Delinquency.* Cambridge, Mass.: Harvard University Press.

Gold, M. 1970. *Delinquent Behavior in an American City.* Belmont, Calif.: Brooks/Cole, Inc.

———. 1977. "Scholastic Experiences, Self-Esteem and Delinquent Behavior: A Theory for Alternative Schools." In *Theoretical Perspectives on School Crime,* edited by R. Z. Emrick. Washington, D.C.: U.S. Department of Health, Education, and Welfare.

Gold, M., and Douvan, E., eds. 1969. *Adolescent Development: Readings in Theory and Research.* Boston, Mass.: Allyn and Bacon.

Gold, M., and Mann, D. 1972. "Delinquency as Defense." *American Journal of Orthopsychiatry* 42:463–79.

Gold, M., and Moles, O., Jr. 1978. "Delinquency in Schools and the Community." In *School Violence,* edited by J. A. Inciardi. Beverly Hills, Calif.: Sage Publications.

Gold, M., and Petronio, R. J. 1980. "Delinquent Behavior in Adolescence." In *Handbook of Adolescent Psychology,* edited by J. Adelson. New York: Wiley-Interscience.

Gold, M., and Reimer, D. 1975. "Changing Patterns of Delinquent Behavior among Americans 13 through 16 Years Old: 1967–72." *Crime and Delinquency Literature* 7:483–517.

Gottfredson, G. D.; Joffe, R. D.; and Gottfredson, D. C. 1981. *Measuring Victimization and the Explanation of School Disruption.* Baltimore: Center for Social Organization of Schools, The Johns Hopkins University.

Gurin, G.; Veroff, J.; and Feld, S. 1960. *Americans View Their Mental Health.* New York: Basic Books.

Hewitt, L. E., and Jenkins, R. L. 1947. *Fundamental Patterns of Maladjustment.* Springfield, Ill.: State Printer.

Hirschi, T. 1969. *Causes of Delinquency.* Berkeley: University of California Press.

Hirschi, T., and Hindelang, M. J. 1977. "Intelligence and Delinquency: A Revisionist Review." *American Sociological Review* 42:571–87.

Hundleby, J. D. 1968. "The Trait of Anxiety as Defined by Objective Performance Measures and Indices of Emotional Disturbance in Middle Childhood." *Multivariate Behavioral Research,* Special Issue, 7–14.

Jenkins, R. L. 1968. "The Varieties of Children's Behavioral Problems and Family Dynamics." *American Journal of Psychiatry* 124:1440–45.

Johnston, L. D. 1973. *Drugs and American Youth.* Ann Arbor: Institute for Social Research.

Johnston, L. D.; O'Malley, P. M.; and Eveland, L. K. 1978. "Drugs and Delinquency: A Search for Causal Connections." In *Longitudinal Research on Drug Use: Empirical Findings and Methodological Issues,* edited by D. G. Kandel. Washington, D.C.: Hemisphere Press.

Kaplan, H. B. 1980. *Deviant Behavior in Defense of Self.* New York: Academic Press.

Kennedy, J.; Mitchell, J. B.; Klearman, L. V.; and Murray, A. 1976. "A Day School Approach to Aggressive Adolescents." *Child Welfare* 55:712–24.

Kifer, E. 1975. "Relationships between Academic Achievement and Personality Characteristics: A Quasi-Longitudinal Study." *American Educational Research Journal* 12:191–210.

Kozol, J. 1980. *The Night Is Dark and I Am Far from Home.* New York: Seabury.

Kulka, R. A.; Mann, D. W.; and Klingel, D. M. 1980. "A Person-Environment Fit Model of School Crime and Disruption." In *Violence and Crime in the Schools: Theoretical Perspectives,* edited by K. Baker and J. Rubel. New York: D. C. Heath.

Lewin, K. 1945. "The Research Center for Group Dynamics at Massachusetts Institute of Technology." *Sociometry* 8:126–36.

McCord, W., and McCord, J. 1959. *Origins of Crime.* New York: Columbia University Press.

McDill, E. L., and Coleman, J. S. 1963. "High School Social Status, College Plans, and Interest in Academic Achievement: A Panel Analysis." *American Sociological Review* 28:905–18.

McKay, H. 1967. "Report on the Criminal Careers of Male Delinquents in Chicago." In President's Commission on Law Enforcement and the Administration of Justice, *Task Force Report: Juvenile Delinquency and Youth Crime.* Washington, D.C.: U.S. Government Printing Office.

Mann, D. W. 1980. "Methodological, Developmental and Sex Biases in the Social Self-esteem Test?" *Journal of Personality Assessment* 44:253–57.

———. 1981. "Age and Differential Predictability of Delinquent Behavior."
    Social Forces 60:97–113.

Mann, D. W., and Gold, M. 1980. *Alternative Schools for Disruptive Second-
    ary Students.* Washington, D.C.: National Institute of Education.

Mann, D. W.; Petronio, R. J.; Gold, M.; and Tomlin, P. 1978. *To Test the
    Effects of Alternative Schools: A Feasibility Study.* Ann Arbor: In-
    stitute for Social Research.

Maruyama, G.; Rubin, R. A.; and Kingsbury, G. G. 1981. "Self-esteem and
    Educational Achievement: Independent Constructs with a Common
    Cause?" *Journal of Personality and Social Psychology* 40:962–75.

Massimo, J., and Shore, M. 1963. "The Effectiveness of a Comprehensive,
    Vocationally Oriented Psychotherapeutic Program for Adolescent De-
    linquent Boys." *American Journal of Orthopsychiatry* 33:634–42.

Matza, D. 1964. *Delinquency and Drift.* New York: Wylie.

Miller, M. O. 1980. "Iatrogenesis in the Juvenile Justice System." Ph.D.
    diss., The University of Michigan.

Moos, R. H. 1974. *Classroom Environment Scale Manual.* Palo Alto: Con-
    sulting Psychologists Press.

Naar, R. 1964. "An Attempt to Differentiate Delinquents from Non-Delin-
    quents on the Basis of Projective Drawings." *Journal of Criminal
    Law, Criminology, and Police Science* 55:107–10.

National Institute of Education (NIE). 1978. *Violent Schools—Safe Schools.*
    Washington: U.S. Department of Health, Education, and Welfare.

Palmore, E., and Hammond, P. 1964. "Interacting Factors in Juvenile De-
    linquency." *American Sociological Review* 29:848–54.

Persons, R. W. 1967. "The Relationship between Psychotherapy with In-
    stitutionalized Boys and Subsequent Community Adjustment." *Jour-
    nal of Consulting Psychology* 31:137–41.

Persons, R. W., and Pepinsky, H. B. 1966. "Convergence in Psychotherapy
    with Delinquent Boys." *Journal of Counseling Psychology* 13:329–34.

Phillips, J. C., and Kelly, D. H. 1979. "School Failure and Delinquency."
    Criminology 17:194–207.

Postman, N., and Weingartner, C. 1969. *Teaching as a Subversive Activity.*
    New York: Delacorte.

Prendergast, M. A., and Binder, D. A. 1975. "Relationships of Selected Self
    Concept and Academic Achievement Measures." *Measurement and
    Evaluation in Guidance* 8:2.

Quay, H. C. 1964. "Dimensions of Personality in Delinquent Boys as In-
    ferred from the Factor Analyses of Case History Data." *Child Develop-
    ment* 35:479–84.

Radcliffe, G. S., and Robins, L. N. 1980. "Predictors of Antisocial Behavior."
    International Journal of Mental Health 67:153–62.

Radloff, L. S. 1977. "The CES-D Scale: A Self-Report Depression Scale for
    Research in the General Population." *Applied Psychological Measure-
    ment* 1:385–401.

Randolph, M. H., Richardson, H., and Johnson, R. C. 1961. "A Comparison of Social and Solitary Male Delinquents." *Journal of Consulting Psychology* 25:293–95.

Reckless, W. C., and Dinitz, S. 1972. *The Prevention of Juvenile Delinquency: An Experiment.* Columbus: Ohio State University Press.

Robins, L. N. 1966. *Deviant Children Grown Up.* Baltimore: Williams and Wilkins.

Rosenberg, F. R., and Rosenberg, M. 1978. "Self-esteem and Delinquency." *Journal of Youth and Adolescence* 7:279–94.

Rosenberg, M. 1965. *Society and the Adolescent Self-Image.* Princeton, N.J.: Princeton University Press.

Rosenshine, B., and Furst, N. 1973. "The Use of Direct Observation to Study Teaching." In *Second Handbook of Research on Teaching,* edited by R. N. W. Travers. Chicago: Rand McNally.

Rubel, R. J. 1977. *The Unruly School: Disorders, Disruptions and Crimes.* Lexington, Mass.: D. C. Heath.

Schab, F. 1968. "Adolescence in the South: A Comparison of White and Negro Attitudes about Home, School, Religion, and Morality." *Adolescence* 3:33–38.

Shinohara, M., and Jenkins, R. L. 1967. "MMPI Study of Three Types of Delinquents." *Journal of Clinical Psychology* 23:128–32.

Shore, M. F., and Massimo, J. L. 1966. "Comprehensive Vocationally Oriented Psychotherapy for Adolescent Delinquent Boys: A Follow-up Study." *American Journal of Orthopsychiatry* 36:609–15.

———. 1969. "Five Years Later: A Follow-up Study of Comprehensive Vocationally Oriented Psychotherapy." *American Journal of Orthopsychiatry* 39:769–73.

———. 1973. "After Ten Years: A Follow-up Study of Comprehensive Vocationally Oriented Psychotherapy." *American Journal of Orthopsychiatry* 43:128–32.

———. 1979. "Fifteen Years after Treatment: A Follow-up Study of Comprehensive Vocationally Oriented Psychotherapy." *American Journal of Orthopsychiatry* 49:240–45.

Shore, M.; Massimo, J. L.; Mack, R.; and Malasky, C. 1968. "Studies of Psychotherapeutic Change in Adolescent Delinquent Boys: The Role of Guilt." *Psychotherapy: Theory, Research and Practice* 5:85–88.

Short, J. F., and Strodtbeck, F. L. 1965. *Group Process and Gang Delinquency.* Chicago: University of Chicago Press.

Smith, V. H. 1974. *Alternative Schools.* Lincoln, Neb.: Professional Educators Publications.

Spielberger, C. D.; Gorsuch, R. L.; and Lushene, R. E. 1970. *Manual for the State Trait Anxiety Inventory.* Palo Alto: Consulting Psychologists Press.

Stern, G. 1970. *People in Context.* New York: Wiley.

Swidler, A. 1976. "What Free Schools Teach." *Social Problems* 24:214–27.

Trickett, E. J., and Moos, R. H. 1973. "Social Environment of Junior and

High School Classrooms." *Journal of Educational Psychology* 65:93–102.

――――. 1974. "Personal Correlates of Contrasting Environments: Student Satisfaction in High School Classrooms." *American Journal of Community Psychology* 2:1–12.

Weinberg, C. 1964. "Achievement and School Attitudes of Adolescent Boys as Related to Behavior and Occupational Status of Families." *Social Forces* 42:462–66.

West, D. J., and Farrington, D. P. 1973. *Who Becomes Delinquent?* London: Heinemann Educational Books.

Williams, J. R., and Gold, M. 1972. "From Delinquent Behavior to Official Delinquency." *Social Problems* 20:2.

Williams, R. L., and Cole, S. 1968. "Self-concept and School Adjustment." *Personnel and Guidance Journal* 46:478–81.

Wylie, R. 1974. *The Self Concept.* Rev. ed. Lincoln: University of Nebraska Press.

Ziller, R.; Hagey, J.; Smith, M.; and Long, B. 1969. "Self Esteem: A Self-Social Construct." *Journal of Consulting and Clinical Psychology* 33:84–95.

Index

Academic prospects, 58, 70, 71, 92, 113, 131, 135, 151, 153–54; and attitude toward school, 118–22; and flexibility of school, 108; measure of, 98

ACE, 43; comparison group for, 74–76; description of, 43–48; effect on parent-adolescent relations, 144; effects of, 127–32; referrals to, 73–74

Adjustment, 88, 91–94; measures of, 20, 96

Age of students, 76, 87, 90–91, 112; and delinquent behavior, 76

Aggression, 25

Alpha, 33; comparison group for, 77–79; description of, 33–36; effect on parent-adolescent relations, 144; effects of, 127–32; referrals to, 76–77

Alternative schools, 3, 4; appropriate sites for, 156; effectiveness of, 13–14, 15–17, 70–71, 99–100; as model schools, 158–59; programs, 11–17, 32–35. *See also* ACE; Alpha; Beta; Evening Youth Program

Alternative Schools, 4

Anderson, B. D., 12

Anxiety, 5, 6, 7, 8, 28, 29, 88, 91–94, 95, 99, 110, 112, 131, 152, 154, 161

Arnove, R., 4

Aronson, E., 26

Attitude toward school, 89, 91–94, 96, 99, 130–31, 135, 139, 144, 146, 151, 155; and academic prospects, 118–22; and commitment to the student role, 118–22; and disruptive behavior, 123–26; measures of, 97–98

Attrition. *See* Response rates

Authority, 8, 25

Bachman, J. G., 10, 20, 26, 88, 96, 146, 154

Behavior modification, 4, 15

Bennet, V. D., 20

Benning, J. J., 22

Berman, S. M., 24

Beset-buoyant index, 110; reliability of, 110–11

Beset students, 99, 152; and changes in each program, 127–30; characteristics of, 112–13; defined, 110; treatment of, 160–62

Beta, 36; comparison groups for, 79–80; description of, 36–38; effect on parent-adolescent relations, 144; effects of, 127–32; referrals to, 79–80

Bills' Index of Adjustment, 20

Binder, D., 20

Bledsoe, J. C., 20

Bowman, P. H., 13, 140

Brooks, G. H., 20

Buoyant students, 152; and changes in each program, 127–30; characteristics of, 112–13; defined, 110

California Achievement Test, 20

Campbell, D. T., 162

Center for Epidemiological Studies Depression Scale, 97, 110

Classroom affect, 58, 67. *See also* Teacher-student relations, measure of, 56

Classroom Environment Scale, 56

Classroom maintenance, 67

Classroom observations, 62–68; and correlations with teacher-student relations, 67–68